Dieter Mittelsten Scheid · In the Mirror of Silence

Dieter Mittelsten Scheid

In the Mirror
of Silence

nicolai

For further information on new editions at Nicolai Verlag
please visit our website and facebook page.

www.nicolai-verlag.de

nicolai *Der Hauptstadtverlag*

© 2013 Nicolaische Verlagsbuchhandlung GmbH, Berlin
© Photography: Dieter Mittelsten Scheid and Batya Schwartz

Translation into English and revision: Dieter Mittelsten Scheid and Batya Schwartz
Copy-editing: June Inderthal
Production: Christine Noack

Printed in the EU

ISBN 978-3-89479-787-4

TABLE OF CONTENTS

BRIDGES FOR DAILY LIFE

APPENDIX

ACKNOWLEDGEMENTS

It is my heart-felt wish to express through this book my profound appreciation for all beings, people and influences that have supported, stimulated and enriched me, and for life itself as it manifests, always anew, in its abundant wonders.

My deep gratitude goes to all those who have been and are close to me, for what they gave to me and what they conveyed to me: my mother, my father, my son, my grandparents, my sister, my family, my friends, my teachers and many others. Above all I want to thank my wife, Batya, for her continuous loving support, inspiration and enduring patience. Like a precious mirror she encouraged me to genuinely re-examine what I was attempting to express and to remain authentic. Without her engagement and her ongoing collaboration during the silence retreats – without her being – this book would never have been written, and would have never been translated into English.

My thanks go especially to all those who participated in our silence retreats during the past 30 years. In silently meeting one another and in being together, significant insights were revealed to me that found their expression in this book. In addition, I am grateful for the many individual talks with friends and the meditative dialogues in our groups where we explored together essential existential subjects and questions, confronting and stimulating each other throughout the years.

I have been influenced by many writers and thinkers in the areas of natural and cognitive science, philosophy and religion, as well as poetry, all of whom contributed to shaping my way of observing, sensing and experiencing. It is impossible for me to name all of them here. And as it does not correspond to my direct way of writing to quote from other authors, I include a list of works in the appendix that were especially relevant for me in the context of writing this book. I wish to emphasize my deep appreciation to all of these authors.

I would like to express my great respect and love for Jiddu Krishnamurti, whose humanness and teachings had a great impact on my life. He taught me to understand the processes of our human consciousness and thinking, and to discover the secrets of the Now.

Lastly, I want to thank the entire team of Nicolai Verlag in Berlin for their deep commitment to creating this book. I am especially grateful to Freia Schleyerbach who did her utmost to accommodate my wishes. Our collaboration was a real joy for me.

Dieter Mittelsten Scheid, Radda in Chianti, Spring 2013

PREFACE TO THE ENGLISH EDITION

This book was originally written and published in German. In the course of translating the text into English – with the unwavering support, input and help of Batya Schwartz – many parts were changed. New texts were added and others omitted. Since the subjects dealt with are often difficult to describe with words and as it is challenging to translate poetry, we encountered various difficulties and gained many insights into language. New formulations of meanings often had to be considered. In many respects, the English version of the book is, therefore, quite different from the original German one.

There are a few key words in the German text which have connotations for which we found no equivalent in the English language. The German word "Anwesenheit", for instance, can mean "the essential being of something is present". We translated it as "presence" which is also the translation for the German word "Präsenz". The English word "present" is in German "Gegenwart". While "presence" and "present" seem to have similar meanings, "Anwesenheit" and "Gegenwart" have very different connotations. Therefore, it might be helpful for understanding certain parts of the book to bear in mind that when using the word "present" I am referring to the Now, whilst the word "presence" refers to the "living essence" that manifests in the Now.

It is beyond our capacity and our intention to enter into a linguistic discourse here. The translation process basically taught us how relative and subjective our words and their individual meanings are. By not taking words too seriously or adhering to their literal meaning, we see them like a dance, a transient art form, a flight of the mind: before and after them, silence and the unknown reign.

The translation process was accompanied from beginning to end by Kevin Mutschler who continuously made valued corrections and suggestions, and gave a significant editing touch to the text. I am deeply grateful for his contributions. Above all, I appreciated the way in which he resonated with the content of the book, supporting and encouraging me throughout this journey.

I wish to end this preface by extending my profound gratitude to my editor, June Inderthal, for her valuable engagement in editing the text. Through her sensitive and intelligent understanding of the presented material and her impressive mastery of the English language, she has enhanced the book with linguistic clarity and beauty.

INTRODUCTION

Weightless these words,
as they come and go.
Like blossoms
they fall.
Like shooting stars
they glow away
in the dark.

AN INVITATION

This book is an invitation to walk together with me on a path of listening and to look into the mirror of silence, where we will find ourselves.

It is a personal book, recounting an inner search, an exploration into the depth of our humanness as it manifests in all its conditional forms and into the immeasurable beauty of our being. It is an attempt to come close to the fire of aliveness itself, the fire which enables us to breathe, perceive, think and be creative, and to find the light-source within us through which we appear and act in the world as unique beings.

Stimulated mainly by the teachings of J. Krishnamurti and Sri Nisarga-datta Maharaj, as well as by the mystical writings of Meister Eckhart, Dschelaleddin Rumi and others, I followed for many years an inner call to find out, through direct and personal experience, the real meaning of their words and messages. Why do they insist that we are asleep and are living in a dream? What does it mean that the observer is the observed, and that only the Now is real? And, if my identity is indeed illusive, who then am I?

The book reflects my experiences and discoveries on this never-ending path of attentive listening. For many years I have regularly spent weeks with-out talking, retreating into nature either alone or with other people. These silent periods have always been the most precious part of the year for me. They have led me into a deep and direct contact with the wonders of nature, and have offered me the rare opportunity to observe, attentively, the inner processes of thinking, feeling and sensing. Being profoundly moved, inspired and enriched by these retreats, I often felt a spontaneous call to share my experiences and to find ways of communicating them to others.

This book is the outcome of that call. My hope is that the detailed descriptions of my perceptions, emotions and their accompanying mental processes – together with my poems – may open some doors and introduce you to possible new paths of self-observation. I wish to arouse your curiosity and pique your interest in experiencing silence, and hope to stimulate you on your own life's journey. At the same time I invite you to question and challenge what you read here and to find out for yourself whether these insights can bring you closer to your own truth. As there is no authority on "truth", one can only find it out for oneself.

The motivation for my inquiry into these questions springs from a puzzling double-aspect of our human existence. We seem to live on the one hand as separate, autonomous individuals with all our specific unique physical and psychological characteristics; at the same time, we are an inseparable part of life's holistic oneness and interconnectedness, where everything moves together and is, essentially, unknowable. This implies that, parallel to the evolving choreography of our personal life-story, there constantly exists another reality which is the very essence of life itself. It is this reality that calls us into the immediate presence of the Now, where our known identity fades away into the background as the wonders of life take us in.

My main intention in writing this book is to inspire you to become more conscious of this double-aspect of our existence and to delve deeper into its paradoxical mystery. I want to share with you my own enthusiasm, as well as my inner struggles, as I explore this eternal mystery. On this path I frequently encountered areas of conflict, confusion and psychic suffering, which often surface when we take our individual personal world to be the only reality, thereby losing direct contact to the actual present. I wish to share with you my insights into these psychological dynamics. Above all, I wish to express my awe and my humble gratitude towards the intelligent and harmonious essence which is continuously creating the rich diversity of our world, with all its myriad realities.

In order to walk together on this path of listening, observing and questioning, I invite you from the very start to ask yourself a most personal question: "What is really important in my life and what are my innermost concerns?"

I encourage you to listen to this question in a quiet place in nature that you love, and if possible, to retreat for a few days to a safe space where you can be alone, free from all schedules and without distractions. If you can, let these days become a creative pause, a time of contemplation, without stress or over-stimulation. Do nothing more than open your senses and your perception, and take in everything that appears inside or outside of you. As you listen patiently to the questions arising from within the mind, without searching for answers, you may notice how the cinema of your emotions and thoughts begins to play before your inner eye. And you may ask yourself: "What is the relationship between these inner personal films and the present moment?"

During the first days it might be difficult for you to be simply present, without involvement in daily programs and without distractions. Our brain is so accustomed to being constantly busy, that we quickly feel edgy if we suddenly have nothing to do. Some of us might even regard it as a waste of time when not doing something "meaningful", even if only for a short while. I want to encourage you to overcome such initial crises and to surrender, despite some inner restlessness to a state of pausing and listening. Only if we let go of the habitual, can we embrace something new.

After some days of silence, as everything surrounding you intensifies, you may feel that something that is as yet unknown begins to touch you. Unexpected answers might emerge, and out of them new questions may be formed. Sometimes you may feel confused, irritated and find yourself searching for a new orientation. At other times you might sink into a deep serenity and become acutely aware that everything occurring around you is happening independently of your own initiative or doing. You may find yourself in the midst of numerous movements and appearances, happening together in consciousness and originating from an unknown source. In such moments, the presence of now may touch you and fill you with a feeling of having arrived back home.

Walking together the path of silence.

No words between us.

And there –

in the middle of all –

we are one.

ABOUT THE STRUCTURE OF THE BOOK

Most of the text of this book was written during silence retreats that I have conducted together with my wife Batya Schwartz over the past 30 years in Poci, our retreat center in Tuscany. To give you a clearer idea about the context in which we have worked and in which the texts came into being, I include in the appendix a short description of the retreat structure and program.

The book begins with descriptions of my concrete personal surroundings, experiences and observations; it goes on to impressions of silent encounters in groups and then focuses on many prevalent questions concerning our selves, our ways of perceiving the world and, finally, our understanding of reality itself. The final part of the book describes the integration of these experiences as we return home after the retreats, with suggestions for a daily practice of awareness.

The book is a compilation of passages and poems drawn mainly from my retreat diaries, which were written spontaneously whenever I felt inspired and moved by new insights. They were drafted, intermittently, throughout the retreat days – at the end of a meditation, during a walk in the woods, following sublime moments by the riverbed or underneath the starry sky. Some entries reflect poetic impressions from such moments in nature, while others are detailed descriptions of observations about processes of the mind that appeared relevant to me. There are also passages which describe inner reflections about broader issues concerning consciousness and the human experience. The interweaving of both prose and poetry, of direct atmospheric impressions and more intellectual reflections, is an attempt to express moods and insights in different forms and at different levels of awareness.

In ordering the texts I was guided by various considerations. I wanted to mirror the constant changes in consciousness which we can observe during the course of a silence retreat – as our attention moves from sensory perceptions to personal or abstract thoughts, and to feelings. I chose to arrange the text in a way that creates a flowing imagery in which different realities are constantly interwoven and dissolved.

The frequent repetitions and paradoxical observations that you will encounter throughout the book are as much a part of this self-discovery process as are the persistent questions: "What is perception? What is the body? What is the 'I'? What is consciousness?" While reading the book I invite you, always, to observe your own patterns of thinking and perceiving, as well as the convictions and values that surface in your awareness. It is an opportunity, to discover, without judgments, some of our blind spots, fixations and automatic habits.

I am aware that words can never fully mirror the ultimate truth and that our attempts to describe "reality" are always relative and limited. Nor can we know whether the words we express are really understood in the way we mean them. Words and statements are always a personal interpretation and are, therefore, never "true". They might, however, point towards something which they themselves do not contain. My spontaneous style of writing may sometimes make it appear that I am describing my personal observations and insights as apparent "facts" or "truths". Occasionally this impression might serve the useful purpose of provoking reactions and questions. I trust, however, that you will not believe my "truths" to be "facts", but that you will rather use them as stimuli on your own path of self-inquiry.

Gentle mind,
now, quiet down.
The silence
clears the clouds away.
The wind meets no restraint.
So tender, fine
this moment now.

Moved deeply by the inner transformations which occur during the retreats, when we are absorbed by the beauty of nature and the immediacy of the Now, I constantly return to one essential question, one which I explore throughout the book: "What is the relationship between our ego and the present moment – the connection between our inner and outer identifications and the immediate presence of being?" During the course of our communal daily activities in the retreat – being in the kitchen, eating or meditating – or while sitting alone by the creek, this question always accompanied me. It was like an open door, inviting my senses to "listen" without having any fixed objective.

This question guided my attention as it alternated between being focused on 'me' to becoming aware of the chorus of all other presently occurring impressions. Eventually, I became more anchored and supported by the present and less dominated by personal issues or attempts to satisfy some desire or to understand and control everything around me. Coming increasingly into contact with the presence and the living essence of each single moment changed my understanding of conflict, of love, compassion, impermanence and death.

May this book bring the question of our relationship to the Now close to you and inspire you to look, with me, into the many mirrors of our existence – reflecting, over and over again, new aspects of our inner and outer realities: dances in consciousness, dances in the wide cosmic space. Maybe then, when we see all the mirrors and their reflections mingle into one, the known worlds might dissolve and transform into a constant flow of the unknown and the unknowable.

You need not be you
in order to be.
The hours,
just passing away,
forget them now.
And yourself as well.

This bustling mind
give to the wind,
and the weight of your soul
to the earth and the sky above.

Not I am the center,
the source of creation.
Nor you,
nor they.

What then, if we too
are losing face?
Let go, let go,
so that it can touch us,
this present being
with its serenity.

ON THE PATH OF SILENCE

TUNING IN

Once again I am in silence! Its unique quality spreads throughout the space, throughout my being. It nourishes and caresses me with its natural beauty as I surrender more and more to the quiet. I feel inspired to write from within this space of silence, hoping to find words that will transport you from wherever you may be right now into your innermost home of simply being.

Silence is a time for the essential. It is a time in which we let ourselves be touched and absorbed by the essence of life. To be taken in by silence is thoroughly wholesome. It feels like coming home. Only then do we become aware of our long absence, of our wandering in remote and foreign lands. Only then do we realize that we have been living inside the walls of our own prison, a prison consisting of our roles and stories, our convictions and indoctrinations – entangled in the world of our ego. We have forgotten how it feels to simply be – without excessive duties, without a function, without having to do anything specific, without having to be anyone special, without wanting anything else – only to be here with what is.

From afar I hear
the wandering wind,
and echoes of rumbling thunder.

Today a sultry wave
of blazing heat.
My brain a vessel,
receiving the wind.

And then a hush
spreads through the space,
silencing all within.
Thoughts fall away.
Too arduous
their way into form.

Somewhere rain.
Its freshness,
its perfume,
rejoicing here.

OBSERVING

As being and writing flow into each other a wordless silence begins to talk.

I am lying in the hammock, looking up, and see layers of leaves and branches interlacing against the blue sky and the play of light. Two movements are mingling together: the slow swaying of the branches and the joyous dance of the leaves. Through a soft, far-looking gaze, everything seems to flicker and melt into one. It is difficult to formulate sentences or to write them down. My eyelids keep closing and my head sinks back. A feeling emerges of a wind blowing gently through the brain – of a soft breeze which empties it while filling it simultaneously with the weightless pleasure of the unknown.

In the afternoon I walk along the riverbed, directly underneath the old mill-house where we live. Here, the water is very calm, broad and deep. Though nearly motionless, the river keeps flowing, on and on. Above it rises a high dome of trees. I love this part of the river. Even in the hottest hours it is cool and offers me peace. Now it is glistening with the magic light of the late afternoon; its water reflecting the golden shine of the leaves and the fresh green moss scattered on rocks. Farther upstream, above a large water basin, a big rock protrudes out of the wooded slope of the left bank. This pool is always deeper and cooler than I imagine. Yet, I jump in. It is so fresh, as if springing directly from its source.

I feel again how the wish to communicate about silence is burning in my heart and is calling for expression. Silence has been for me a treasure revered for many years yet each time discovered completely anew. It asks to be shown to others and moves me to talk about those unexpected moments in which we are led into a space that can be described with the word "paradise" – a paradise that is always there. In a magical way it is healing us – healing us from ourselves.

Sun and thunder together
and the flapping wings of a bird
bathing in the creek.

Alert,
awake,
looking and listening.
Each moment
a new movement,
happening by itself.

The wind, the thunder,
the heated light.
Life is fulfilling itself
and never stands still.

I slow down and everything becomes quieter still. The space is condensed and filled with presence. It is immeasurable, a wide and immense power.

I slow my pace and this presence comes still nearer, dispersing my thoughts. The space in-between becomes perceptible. Vastness breathes through the words, making them faint. Their weight lightens and their meaning fades away.

IDENTITY

The weight and meaning of words – they form a crucial part of our identity. Through thoughts and verbal descriptions, an image of ourselves is created in consciousness, and we believe ourselves to be that image.

When I think 'I', a whole archive of my collected self-portraits is automatically activated from memory. The feeling of 'I' becomes immediately charged with a sense of importance that has developed throughout my entire life-story, consolidating firmly the belief that this is 'me'. And, when I think 'you', 'we' or 'they', other people surface from my memory and appear to be an actual reality.

Subsequently, these specific pictures of 'me' and 'you' start interacting in my imagination. Sometimes the scene evoked is a memory, sometimes a projection into the future, and sometimes pure fantasy. We encounter each other through images moving in our brains and through the sensations these images evoke in our bodies. Through this kind of image production, our lives can be experienced as a vivid film, a film coming from the past, running now in consciousness.

It is morning – the water is still cold and the foot hesitates to step in. The sun shines through the trees that cover the steep slope on the other side of the river. "Is this forest also just an image constructed by the brain?" – The thought is immediately hushed. The reality of the presence is too intense.

But the questions remain: "If I am not an image, who am I really? How do I suddenly appear in consciousness? Whether or not this is a film – am I not here?"

I pass the huge wisteria that covers the old stone wall of the house. It is full with new blossoms in the middle of August, smaller and darker than in the spring when they froze. Big, black-violet fluorescent bumblebees drink from the blossoms alongside countless butterflies. One of them is very small, and only from up close do I notice the fine pastel design of her wings. I think: "She won't ask herself if her beauty is seen, or if it makes any sense to flutter around so inconspicuously in the world."

Only we ask ourselves such questions and evaluate our actions and encounters. How often do we measure, more or less consciously, the correctness of our behavior and self-worth and try to convince ourselves that our life makes sense! How often am I busy with my self-image and my appearance in the world, as if I have nothing better to do! While at that very moment, presence is pervading all and is indivisible. The butterfly, the wisteria, we ourselves, every single thing is imbued with life – with presence. So how does it happen that I experience myself as being a separate 'I' within this indivisible flow of being? And, how did I develop such a secure feeling of certainty and conviction that I am actually moving and acting independently in the world – separate from all else?

PERCEIVING AND THINKING

In slow motion it takes thirty minutes to walk to the place by the river where we meditate. Normally it takes only five. With the slowness of walking, the whole sense of existence intensifies. Even the dry bushes breathe presence and the green of the juniper radiates in its surroundings. In between, fleeting thoughts appear and disappear. Sometimes they solidify into the apparent reality of an inner film or an imagined story, swaying my attention. When presence re-enters and permeates the field of awareness once again, it becomes clear how absent I have just been, and how much energy is needed to remain awake and aware. The inner films consume this energy, and thus easily absorb me into the mists and dreams of my imaginary worlds.

The same thing happens again while sitting in meditation. The stillness comes in waves and bathes the brain. The wind, the songs of the birds and the roebuck's cry; the breath, the pains and the ant on the skin: none of this disturbs the silence, which is deeper and wider than all. Only my thoughts – as they continue to form some "reality" – cover up the inner tranquil state of being and paint images over it. Immediately, the "taste" of consciousness is changed, taking on a distinct "flavor" evoked by the content of the thoughts. Tension and strain are now felt again in the brain, only to dissolve as the thoughts sink back into silence. Then – undisturbed being – until the next image appears.

Breathing in space.
Becoming the space.
Silence spreads.
Inside and outside is one.

BEING BUSY IN OUR MINDS

Being surrounded by the simplicity of nature and immersed in the peaceful-ness of silence, I ask myself: "What is keeping us so busy all the time, often hindering us from being in direct contact with the essence of life during our daily routines?" Are we not spending too much time within the self-made walls of our personal habits and reality bubbles? Do we ever invest the time necessary to find out what really moves us, asking ourselves: "Who are we really?" Or is it that the depth of this question rarely touches us due to the basic conviction that we know who we are and are certain that we are what we know?

SELF-OBSESSION

In observing ourselves honestly, we will notice that we are busy with our-selves most of the time; self-absorbed with who we believe ourselves to be and with what we take to be our world.

At least once, but usually several times a day, we ask ourselves: "How do I look? What do the others think about me? Am I liked? Have I acted stupidly? How attractive am I? Am I too fat? Am I cool enough? Didn't I do this well? Did I make a mistake? Should I have more pride? Why did she or he say this to me and why did they stare at me?"

We ask ourselves whether we are in the right relationship or why we do not have a partner. We wonder if we should change our workplace or learn a different profession: "Why do I fail so often? Why are others better off? How could I strive to become more successful and more liked?"

Or, contrary to the above, we may feel very good about ourselves, praise ourselves, bathe in our self-image and our successes, all the while secretly fearing the end of such self-gratifying periods.

Often we turn to others, seeking their help in trying to solve our problems. We might go to therapy, take part in personal development courses or have a coach, exploring different roads towards success and self-fulfillment. We ask: "Why and how did I become the person I am and what is my position in my family and my workplace? What are my strengths and weaknesses, my re-sources and my potential?"

In addition, our many feelings and emotions play an important part in keeping our minds busy. At times we may descend into deep anxiety and contrive fearful situations in our imagination. We try to understand them, resolve to stop them, only to reconstruct them, over and over again, believing them to be real. At other times we may be overtaken by feelings of aggression which we may regard as either legitimate or unjustified, and are driven to either act them out or put them under control.

The lake of silence
mirrors all.
All is flickering light.

There is also our precious pride and our many feelings of being hurt and of having been mistreated. We are driven by our ambitions, the pressure of competition and the importance of being in the right. And, how crucial it is for us to be special or at least to be acknowledged! This need is often accompanied by our desire for power and the compulsion to make others dependent on us: the desire to manipulate, suppress and control and to have the power to dictate and to decide what is right.

Then there are all of our yearnings, our dreams, our self-pity, our restlessness and our doubts. And there is pleasure, lust, and greed – the pleasure of eating, the lust in sex and the greed for money. For them we are willing to do almost anything. Driven, we seek them day in and day out – always more, more often, faster, bigger, more intense – more of everything and, if possible, without ever stopping!

Certainly, the mind is not only consumed by these basic obsessions. We are also captivated by great ideals, creative thoughts and projects, and the enthusiasm to express ourselves artistically. We invent, we build, we write or paint. An inner fire is flowing into our creations, keeping us going and intensifying our lives.

Parallel to all of this, we are constantly engaged with our immediate surroundings and with society. They demand constant attention: our work with its challenges, its routines and its stress; the family: caring for the children, the ailing parents, the quarrels or fun with the siblings, Christmas, birthdays and holidays, and the grandchildren; sicknesses and material problems; friends and social obligations; vacations and weekends; and the wish to have some fun, to go out, to take a drive or enjoy, at last, a far-away journey.

Add to this our hobbies and different forms of entertainment, all taking place in the colorful landscape of our lives: playing cards, or golf, or watching soccer; jogging and mountain climbing; visiting exhibitions and concerts; gardening; learning an instrument, as well as reading all the interesting books that are around. And then there are the clubs, the music, and the discos, the alcohol and drugs, and, and, and … And, of course, television – watching the news, sports events, family soaps, quiz shows and, once again, the news. There are all the film channels, the newest DVDs and, naturally, the Internet – another e-mail and another one quickly following it, one more piece of information, another Google search, another Facebook communication and one more chat group, a few more blogs and YouTube clips, and finally, of course, the newest video game and, in between, an incoming and outgoing tide of instant messages. We seem to drown in a never-ending consumption orgy and a flood of ever-new temptations.

The mere enumeration of all these activities and self-obsessions is, in itself, exhausting. How much more strained must we feel, doing all of this day in and day out! And how little time remains to ask: "What is really 'real' in my life?"

And still, there is more. As a member of our society, we are also inevitably involved with our nations and their politics, with the challenges of our economy, environmental dilemmas and cultural differences, with issues of poverty, overpopulation, unemployment, social security or social insecurity; not to mention the facts of globalization, terrorism, biotechnology, the arms race, manipulation of the media – and all the noise, all the hectic activities, all the running around from morning to night.

And last but not least, there is our religion reigning over us, promising us a secure hold and knowledge of the innermost secrets of life; telling us what is good and what is bad, and leading us to the ultimate conclusion that we are sinners and penitents and redeemed ones. We tremble and hope as we pray to prevail. And, armed with all our religious convictions, we set out to convert the rest of the world.

Then, unexpectedly, at some point in life, somebody dies. The funeral and the mourning are followed by disputes about the inheritance; all to be forgotten as the years pass by, until our own end finally comes and death takes hold of us.

Should we not be amazed that more people are not asking themselves: "What is happening to mankind? Have we all become insane? Where are we running to? What makes us so driven? Why all this stress?"

The world seems deadened
in the heat of noon.
From nowhere,
an airplane passing.
The roses on the wall
look at me.

Even if at times we do wonder, or at least ponder for a moment, it still does not prevent us from continuing our lives in our conditioned and familiar ways.

There are those of us who go through life feeling quite well most of the time – boasting a great childhood, happy family life and good partnership, successful profession, beautiful holidays and lots of time to do good. We are the ones who are always content and engaged in helping others to be similarly so. At peace with ourselves, we don't have to ask any further questions.

On the other hand, there are those of us who are always discontent and question everything, always feeling that something is wrong and disturbing. We constantly make mistakes or feel that someone is inflicting injustice upon us. We live in torment moving from rage to desperation, to deep and bitter resignation.

Or, are we the ones who simply take it easy, passing from one day to the next like a dream? Everything is cool, everything is right-on, and we refuse to participate in any of the stress. Here a job, there a job, occasionally a trip far away and a joint that ultimately keeps us alive; and the dream, the dream about ourselves.

We are all of these stories and more. There are the so-called hard working ones and the lazy ones, the beauty queens and the ugly ones, the callous types and the sensitive ones, the achievers and the underdogs, the violent and the modest ones, the less intelligent and the super intelligent, the rich and the poor.

Is this what life is?
What is life?

Seeing all of this and being all of it, do we not feel deep inside of us that there is more, more to life than this? Something is missing. In spite of having forgotten what it is, we sense it, yearn for it and search for it.

Fireflies in the night.
On and off their gliding lights.
Mystery forest.
A hundred souls
shine in the dark.
In the water reflected,
they enlighten the heart.

SILENCE AGAIN

At this very moment, silence is everywhere; no inner nor outer talking. Quietness pervades the entire space. I breathe deeply as my gaze follows the swallows gliding high above. Seeing is seeing. Listening is listening. A cool breeze moves the branches of a nearby apple tree; from near and far, coming and going, melodies and the songs of birds. Breathing with the wind, breathing with all my being – now.

The immediacy of now is so real that it can hardly be expressed with words. The presence of life is silent and yet it talks through all. All sounds, all forms, both visible and invisible, are totally alive here and now, breathing the essence and radiating the presence in simply being.

Words cannot touch this most precious essence that constantly surrounds us and fills us – moving with us wherever we go. Where words are not, silence is. Silence has space. Silence is space. It is the space that holds all. It is our home.

Without words, the brain is quiet. Whatever touches the senses touches the brain – the coolness of the wind on the skin, the voices of people far off in the fields, laughter, insects, a banging door. Inhaling, exhaling – the body relaxes. Beingness is.

Whatever we might say, whatever we read or hear, whatever we think is meaningless here, where the light of this moment shines; this moment, which has never been before and will never be again.

Having this home is all we need – a place, always safe, where we belong and can be, can be who we are. This home takes us in and says "yes".

Here is my home, where I am right now. Its vital being carries me and nothing stands still.

THE 'I'

Whatever our situation – rich or poor, happy or unhappy, man or woman – one characteristic is common to each of us: we are deeply convinced that we are the one who we know as 'I'. When somebody asks us: "Who are you?" our answers will be based on this conviction. We will describe our childhood, our background and family, our biography, our training and work, our partnership and our children, our friendships and relationships, our health and our ailments, our strengths and weaknesses, successes and failures, adventures and journeys. We will talk about our beliefs, our hopes and fears, our likes and dislikes, our relationship to sex and to food, our dependencies, behaviour patterns and so on.

In spite of all the different cultural backgrounds and traditions that have influenced us, most of us will describe ourselves in the above terms, convinced that we are talking about a personal self and about our own individual life without realizing that, in fact, we are recounting nothing other than a story. This belief in the 'I' serves as the solid foundation which supports our identity and upon which we lean.

But, is not this conviction also the foundation of our imprisonment – the imprisonment of the whole of society and of humanity? Are we not held prisoner inside the walls of identities and roles which forever separate us from each other? Are we not leading a life in which we are held in bondage to the very knowledge about ourselves and our world – confined within the shared illusions that mankind has developed and held dear for thousands of years? Have we become so accustomed to our convictions that we cannot recognize them as the building blocks of our self-made prison?

REALITY WORLDS

Two silver-grey butterflies, meeting on the petals of a purple blossom. Self-forgotten they are, drinking the nectar together.

All at once, one flutters away to a nearby flower. Now apart, they are still unified in silence.

TWO STATES OF BEING

Being in silence, we can clearly observe two different "reality-worlds" in which we mainly exist – two reality spheres that appear to have little to do with one another. One is the world of the 'me' with its social and cultural networks of relationships and conditionings. The other is the world of the immediate Now, the living presence of being. I exist simultaneously in two completely different ways: as a biographical, ego-centred identity, and as a present embodiment of the breath of life. The first world consists mainly of thinking and thought-generated emotions and actions. The second consists of the present essence. The first world is made up of what we know and has a past. The second is always new and, ultimately, unknowable.

Living together with others in silence, surrounded by a natural and protective environment, offers an ideal opportunity to experience and explore the distinct realities of these two spheres of existence. Significant questions regarding identity, perception and the process of experiencing inevitably arise. These questions are mirrored each time we encounter one another, and dissolve again into the immediacy of the moment, where our identities dance within the dance of existence.

Crusts are formed,
enclosing the essence –
the masks of personality.
Masks and shells,
the dressage of the world.

LIVING TOGETHER WITHOUT WORDS

Once we stop talking, many of our conventional and habitual patterns of behavior end. In itself, that is enough to transform the reality of whatever we perceive in and around us to an amazing degree. As our contact with others is no longer dominated by words, we see and recognize one another in an entirely new way. We stop meeting each other through the stories that we tell: the episodes of our lives, our trips and love affairs, our professional and family encounters, our worries, problems and convictions, along with the myriad memories that normally come up in our conversations. Being in silence, we cannot draw the other's attention to the personal movies of our struggles and pleasures, evoking the usual array of feelings and associations which carry us far away from the present moment. Discussions about opinions, people, new trends and interesting news or discoveries are no longer possible.

In spending considerable time together without ever speaking a single word, how do we, then, experience each other?

In silence, we express and communicate our state of being directly. We meet being to being – through our eyes, our mimics, our ways of moving and with the mood and energy that we radiate. Naturally, in spite of the silence, we continue to create personal stories about these encounters within ourselves. The difference is that now we are aware that all these stories are creations of our own minds, and we no longer believe them to be an apparent objective reality, as we so often do during our normal verbal exchanges. Though the stories may still be floating as one's own productions in the immediacy of the encounter, they become more transparent and, as they lose their hypnotic potency, they tend to separate us less and less.

It is remarkable to see the consequences of refraining from the habit of constantly explaining, asserting or defending oneself. In silence we are, and can only be, the way we are. We can no longer hide behind our words. We become, therefore, more visible. After an initial phase of feeling insecure, we soon learn to be more accepting. We see each other's uniqueness, our own idiosyncrasies, our vulnerability and, above all, our beauty. In a mysterious way, everyone becomes more lovable.

There are no words

to describe

this very moment.

INNER THOUGHT PROCESSES

What are we thinking while we are not talking?

We think about all manner of things. We think about all the little activities which we plan to do during the day. And, while we do them, we accompany them with inner commentaries. We often describe ourselves in those actions, either with judgments or appraisal. In between, we hold inner dialogues with, or about, the other participants, evaluating them as well – feeling amusement, anger or maybe compassion. We spend a substantial amount of time pondering actual problems and conflicts in our own lives and developing all sorts of feelings towards them. In our minds, we run through possible solutions. And, once we find one, we question it again, and the merry-go-round starts anew.

Frequently, people close to us appear in our minds, and a dialogue with them develops in which we feel appreciation and love, or hurt and rage. Such inner dialogues can last for hours, during which we have intense inner discussions, write long letters or even recite speeches.

At times, utterly senseless images and thoughts can take shape in our minds. They appear out of the blue, make a few circles, like a spinning top,

and give way to the next one. Generally, we don't notice the beginning of a thought sequence and unexpectedly find ourselves in a jungle of arbitrary emotions and inner pictures. Suddenly we are in the midst of an extremely intense personal film, while all along, we are lying in the hammock next to the flowing river.

In this way, we are constantly describing and defining ourselves with changing colors and from different standpoints. Thought talks to itself and to me about 'me'. As we are so accustomed to this inner rhetoric, it might take some time until we question its validity. It may never occur to us that, through thinking, we are constantly creating and re-creating ourselves.

While all these processes unfold in our brains, we are, simultaneously, immersed in the actual sounds and movements of nature. Our body is here, breathing and sensing. We are on this earth which carries us. Above is the sky, surrounding us with its infinite space. As the silent days progress, we become increasingly aware of the striking contrast between the peace and harmony of each present moment and our mechanical and obsessive thinking which so often brings about conflicts and confusing entanglements.

Yet, the worlds of thought which absorb us are not always disturbing or conflicting. Frequently they are filled with inspiration, enthusiasm and beauty. Vibrant new ideas are surfacing and deeply moving insights emerge. Creative energy flows into developing future projects, having profound philosophical revelations, reading or writing intuitive poetry or becoming fascinated and inspired by the thoughts of other authors.

And then, unavoidably, come days of boredom when we no longer know what to do with ourselves and are not attracted by anything. We question everything, and whatever comes to mind seems to be senseless. Nonetheless, even on such days, we do not cease to describe our moods, ourselves and the others.

Looking closely at these thought processes and inner dialogues, it becomes clear that they constitute the basis of our subjective experiences. We become aware that we live most of the time in an "ego-palace" – in a constructed reality made up of stories, from past to future, and interpretations which perpetually isolate us from our immediate environment. As we continue to observe, we come to see and feel acutely how this "ego-palace" inhibits our ability to notice and sense where we actually are – in a space that breathes with the freshness and innocence of life, in which our individual stories are irrelevant and the 'I' is none other than the sense of being itself. Here, life in itself is *I am*.

I ask myself with growing curiosity: "What causes the mind to continuously move between the peacefulness of the one state of being and the confusion and hypnotic attraction of the other?"

LIKE CHILDREN AGAIN

Now and then we are like children who beam and marvel, having returned to our original state of being where we are without knowledge and are only witnessing.

No words can explain why I am filled with such bliss when I sit for long periods of time on top of a rock by the river. As I listen attentively to the water, its sound fills all space and pervades my innermost being. Suddenly, all conflicts, desires and problems vanish inside the water and its flowing music.

And at times, without a reason or a specific thought, I am surprisingly flooded by amazing joy. The conscious mind is infused with serenity, light and inner laughter. The word "happiness" appears, and everything is beautiful in this state. Here, even pain has its place in one's heart. It is as if this joy is able to absorb everything just as it is. Unshakeable joy!

It seems so easy to just "be". It seems so natural to simply sit and to look. I feel I have arrived. Everything that is, is here. Nothing calls me into another space. Nothing pulls me and nothing pushes me. The need to describe myself, the need to be someone known, has disappeared. The taste of presence becomes so much more intense and real as my self-descriptions fade away, dissolving into the Now.

The eyes close and the visual universe disappears. A new cosmos is forming, a new cosmos of now. From outside – nature playing music; from inside – flowing feelings and sensations; the body – a stream carried by breath. And slowly, from nowhere, a space beyond the senses opens up; a space unknown – the mystery behind all.

THE NEED TO BE SOMEONE

One of the most strenuous aspects of our lives is that most of the time we feel compelled to be "someone". This necessity to be somebody, with a defined identity, was taught to us throughout our social upbringing. Our self-image can be seen as a pre-fixed form which we gradually learn to inhabit, until we ultimately become one with it. This ego-form literally materializes in the body, expressing itself in adopted mimics, gestures and postures, rigidifying into a physical 'me' as the years go by. We spend an enormous amount of energy maintaining these ego-formations, especially when difficulties arise in our personal affairs, or when we have to prove that we are in the right and want to prevail. It is then that formed identity solidifies until we become as hard as cement.

What a relief then, during these quiet, silent days, to be free of the need to be "somebody" for a while! Many burdens fall away. Neither tasks nor duties bind or blind us, and we have nothing to justify, to explain or to prove. How wonderful it feels to relax! In amazement, we realize how strenuous life has been until now.

For a few moments, all thinking quietens down. Perceptions and sensations merge inside the all-encompassing space of creation. Nothing is fixed. No holding onto. Everything is born out of deep stillness and sinks back into it; a swirling creative movement in infinite space.

A CONSTRUCTED REALITY

A startling thought surfaces from within: "Can it be that, like the 'I', the world which we perceive and experience is also a constructed reality which only seems to be solid, constant and continuous?" Since it is only in the brain that the images of our "known" world are formed, how can we know what is really out there? How can we prove that separate objects exist that have nothing to do with us? Are we not merely assuming that the world, with all its appearances, is an objective reality totally independent of us?

Is it not more honest and even courageous to simply admit that we know nothing for certain? I do not know what is inside or outside of me. I do not know if you or I are really what we believe ourselves to be. I do not know if this body actually exists or if it is just an appearance that flashes up in consciousness, changing from one moment to the next. I clearly do not know.

Clouds of words,
clouds of pictures,
clouds from beliefs
in our importance –
they dissolve.

Space,
the space.
All is space.

With amusement, I imagine what may be passing through our minds while we silently meditate together by the creek. Personal thoughts, images and emotions are inwardly circulating, while each one of us sits within our own reality-bubble, watching them come and go. How much seriousness and blind belief do we invest and waste in them! And then – the wind and the river and the sudden stillness blow them all away.

In the rolling thunder,
we watch together
as the grass grows.

PERCEPTION IS ACTION

I am swinging in the hammock-seat – moving backwards into the shadow, moving forwards into the heat of the sun. Scraps of thought distract the awareness – and then again, pure listening: from far away, the noise of an airplane – and the river – ever quieter. Nothing but looking.

Krishnamurti always said: "Perception is action." And how true this is! It is as if the purity of listening is carrying me right into the wind which is now blowing. Right now, 'my' being and sensing are the wind. The breeze itself and 'my' perception of it are united, unseparated by comments.

The wind and I, we are one. The activity of life is aware of itself.

There is no distinction between the observer and the observed; they are two aspects of the same – manifesting simultaneously, dissolving simultaneously. The thinker, too, who thinks thoughts and uses these to describe the perceived world, does not exist as a separate entity. Thinker, thinking, and thought, are born together and pass away together. They are one.

Suddenly a swarm of butterflies appears, orange-red with black dots. With greedy thirst they take up water from the pinnate leaves, swaying on top of them. They are completely absorbed with drinking when, all at once, the wind chases them away.

SELF-WORTH

While I continue to observe how the sense of 'me' re-emerges again and again, I notice how deeply connected this process is to our inner pursuit of self-worth. It seems that a sense of worthiness and self-esteem is a basic drive and building block of the ego. Can it be that without positive or negative self-descriptions, the 'I' would no longer have a measurable value and would, therefore, be without weight? Is it possible that the constant activity of defining and judging ourselves could become playful and quite meaningless once we recognize this weightlessness?

A thought takes shape, telling me that somebody is making appreciative remarks about my writing. I hear imagined comments as formulated sentences. My sense of self-worth and self-importance is immediately charged with a feeling of elation and pride – until the whole scenario is exposed as pure fantasy. I have to laugh, and the scene dissolves in the song of the crickets.

Experiencing itself as a separate entity, the 'I', or ego strives obsessively to be in the right, to feel appreciated and worthy and to secure a sense of belonging. It seems to achieve this through drawing clear boundaries around its identity and by polarization: 'my' family, 'my' nationality, 'my' religion, or even 'my' sports club as against 'yours' or 'theirs'.

Our whole mental and physical apparatus reacts automatically the moment we anticipate an appraisal or apprehend an offence concerning our self-image and our identifications. In the event of rejection, our balance and equilibrium become shaky, and we feel immediately threatened. Our tendencies for self-preservation are awakened and we react with a counter attack, a defense or self-doubt. In extreme situations, it is like a survival reflex that instantly seeks any form of stabilization.

The aim is always to feel okay, to belong and to be in harmony with the familiar environment. An apparent sense of security develops, which seems to bring us closer to the feeling of being in unity with life. But, a conditioned security such as this is most likely based on fiction and can easily lose its stability. As the 'I', we can never be completely sure about our self-worth and our belonging, and, therefore, have to stand our ground in each situation anew. How much effort do we have to invest in order to feel liked, loved and valued, only for it all to be challenged once again a moment later, bringing with it total insecurity.

TIME IS PASSING

Time in silence is flying by. While watching, sensing and being attentive, the days slip away. Soon a week has already passed. Without noticing it, my entire rhythm has changed, becoming slower, more natural and at ease. I feel more connected with my body, and it shows me directly what it needs or wants. Any kind of pressure now feels unnatural. Without being pushed or driven, the brain functions in a clear, calm and creative way.

Deep insights come from nowhere and illuminate the basic interconnectedness that underlies what appear to be complex issues and relationships. Surprising solutions for problems, which before seemed so difficult, are now effortlessly revealed. A sense of ease has taken over my whole being.

*Light
is the flight
of the dragonfly.
Ah –
she is gone.*

EVENING MEDITATION

From time to time the drone of two Indian tanpuras, played by my wife, accompanies the evening meditations. They weave a sound-fabric of unworldly harmonies, gentle and rich. Circling waves of sounds, coming and going, form a floating carpet. It carries us. It cradles us. It reminds us. It is the hum of the cosmos – bringing our inner being into resonance. Deep inside, we recognize it as the song of our home.

FORM-CREATION

I cannot stop marvelling at how living forms develop and grow. Reaching out from the corner of the house, an extended branch of a climbing rose balances and dances lightly in the soft wind. I have been observing it with fascination for several weeks. As it grows longer, it continuously winds in new directions. Out of nothing, its form is created in space. It is precisely the right form, with its variety of larger and smaller leaves and the slowly developing buds at the end of its twining branches. Even its many different shades of green are in accordance with an inner order that is unique to the rose.

What incredible intelligence expresses itself in this order! With the help of the elements, this miraculous structure appears in the light, rising out of the unformed and hidden. Wondrous and ungraspable, transforming the invisible into the visible, life is manifesting itself!

Thought-forms dance superficially in the space of awareness, like water ripples upon a deep, wide lake. No matter how important they appear, the forms of the ripples are arbitrary. It is always water and always a lake. The blindness of the 'I' consists in its not seeing or sensing that it itself is of "water" – the water of life.

Each moment
the world materializes anew.

At the bottom
nothing moves.

Over there,
behind the sun,
beyond the glare
surrounding us,
hidden darkness
devouring all.
The vastness of power,
unknown.

BEING AND EGOCENTRICITY

The body is filled with the awareness of presence. Everything is peaceful, awake and happily light. Nothing has to be done or achieved. All is present as it is, and whatever enters consciousness radiates sublime beauty. Happening in unison, everything is perfect and complete. The song of the nightingale comes and goes.

Such peaceful moments are shattered for me when suddenly, and without reason, I remember and envision aspects of our lives that are deeply disturbing. The world of politics or economics enters my mind as well as negative tendencies in my personal life. I feel deeply affected by our capacity to harm each other, mostly out of egotism, greed, power and ideological intolerance. There is such an enormous amount of injustice, brutal suppression and terror in our world! There is so much manipulation, corruption and recklessness! In those moments, it seems incredible to me to realize how insensitive, blind, and immured in self-righteousness we human beings can be!

It seems that all too often, success and power in our society go hand in hand with strong ideological convictions that hinder and then block any direct contact with the presence. It is no wonder that so many of our leaders, rulers and opinion managers seem to be cut off, to a high degree, from life itself and in that way, appear to remain untouched by the global injustice and cruelty facing us all.

And yet, if I am honest, I recognize many of these tendencies in myself as well as in the people who are close to me. This shocks me even more. We shut our eyes to so many facts. We conveniently refuse to really look and to inquire. How often, for example, do we ignore and hurt others for the sake of our own self-interest? Do we not all need to deal with our shadows which we repeatedly try to conceal, but which, nonetheless, manifest themselves in our daily interactions? How often am I intolerant, impatient or angry! How often do I avoid being touched by the worries of my neighbors and develop a numbing indifference towards the many injustices surrounding me!

In the space of silence with its sublime beauty, I suffer more consciously from these painful insights into myself. In seeing how alienated and cut off we all can become, the question arises in me once again with renewed urgency: "How can we bring these two realities together? Which road leads from there to here, from egocentricity into being?"

Evening meditation.
The full moon
in a lake of light.
Colorful clouds,
illuminated.
And below,
dark shadows
of sleeping trees.

OBSERVATIONS

PERCEPTION AND ACTION WITHOUT A 'ME'

Only a limited part of all that is perceived can be identified and abstracted mentally and, in this way, transformed into 'my' personal experience. The larger part of all perceptible movements and happenings is not captured by descriptions or definitions, but appears directly in consciousness without a commentator or an observer.

While walking early in the morning through the meadow, a verbal description appears in my mind of the beauty of the dewdrops on the blades of grass: "How beautifully they glitter in their gold and rainbow colors." At the very same time, all the other phenomena surrounding me pass directly through the conscious space of perception without any intervening description on my part: the different foliage and flowers, the stone slabs and the walls of the house, people sitting here and there, the wooded slope above the river, the sounds of insects, clouds above and the all-encompassing sense of infinite space.

These two components in perception are equally important: the specific detailed phenomena which we focus upon and define, and the complete undivided, surrounding field of impressions that enters consciousness as if through osmosis. One cannot separate them as foreground and background, because the particular and the whole are complementary and constantly intermingle with each other. It seems that attention is simply roaming from one detail to the next: for instance, from crickets chirping to the sounds of water and then to thought content. But, in fact, both focussed and unfocussed impressions are unceasingly interacting and mixing together in the conscious manifestation of each moment.

That which is perceived does not need to be recognized through defining descriptions in order for perception to be conscious and leave its traces in memory. In other words, commented perception is only one aspect of the totality of what is perceived. Were it otherwise, we would not be able to act without thinking, as we so often do while we walk, eat, dress or drive a car. In such thought-free interplay of perception and activity, no observing or commenting 'I' is involved. Appropriate action takes place by itself and happens in precise accordance with the relevant elements of a given situation.

For instance, when somebody taps my shoulder from behind, my body turns spontaneously around and my face reacts before any thoughts of recognition have formulated. Or, while driving a car, an unforeseen danger occurs, prompting the foot to press the brake-pedal immediately before any ego-activity interferes with the situation.

The thought-projected 'I' is like a film running parallel to the actual event. I plan, for example, to walk to the meditation place and bring along an apple to eat. Though the 'I' might decide the beginning and direction of these activities, the concrete and physical coordination processes for these specific actions are always determined by the body's inner knowledge and the nature of the given circumstances. Walking along the path or chewing the apple – in themselves complex processes – are actions carried out by the body itself and its intelligence, and not through the control of my 'I'.

A floating state
between all – in all.

Inter-being.
Out of nowhere
you appear.
Where do we meet,
with our fleeting glances?

The spark of a moment,
a vibrant ray.
And again –
alone with oneself.

The space in between.
There, where we merge,
in mysterious darkness.

THOUGHT AND STILLNESS

During today's meditation, specific thought contents intermingle with a direct sense of the whole. The fathomless space of unquestioned stillness is all around and has its impact on me, even when the attention is not focussed upon it. Simultaneously, while the stillness abides, thoughts run their course – coming and going – from lofty ones to those loaded with meaning.

The concept of thought and silence being opposites and incompatible with each other is misleading. It leads us to a dead-end road, especially when thought tries to silence itself, in order to enter into stillness with the 'I'. This can only be an illusion, since thinking is already taking place inside the infinite space of Now and in the aliveness of being. Thought is already there, at a place that it strives to reach.

The purpose of meditation is not, therefore, to stop thinking in order to be with the Now. The aim is rather to experience thinking as an integral part of the actual life movement and to feel the "taste of Now" in our thoughts. In that instant, a breeze of aliveness blows through all mental content and the Now breathes through every word.

Thinking and non-thinking are not in opposition. Speech and silence do not contradict each other. In the intervening space, where attention is unfocussed and where thinking, discerning and sensing exist side by side, duality no longer exists. It is revealed to be a deception. Everything floats in harmony.

The path leads inside,
into space without form.

Outside the storm,
the raging of time.
But here,
only attention,
the doorway
towards infinity.

All breathing,
all sounds
are silenced
in the stillness
of stillness.

Wide open,
vastness,
no word.

OUR ESSENCE

As the days of silence progress we become highly sensitive and come closer to feeling the essence of our being. We experience *that* we are here rather than *how* we are here. Behind the known identity and the familiar 'I' with its history, its self-image and its conditioned tendencies, the true self is slowly unveiled as the vital core which is unquestionably present and in direct contact with life. In a natural way, we awaken to all that is here: the water, the green surrounding us, the songs of the birds, the people and the great wide space which is within all and contains all. It is a relationship of love in which everything touches everything else, bathing in mutual beauty. Everything is unified in light.

Days pass by and we dare to appreciate this all-embracing presence in each other, too, and to truly meet one another, being to being. In such moments, our personal history is no longer in the foreground of our encounters. Rather, we see each other afresh, feeling recognized in our essence. Being together in such a unified way does not erase the diversity of our individual features. Rather, they merge and interweave within the tapestry of the whole.

Having become more sensitive, we now have an acute perception of how certain stereotypical behavior patterns have been engraved in the body; and how the body, in turn, has become imprisoned within them. We feel in ourselves and see in others how strenuous and even agonizing this process can be. And yet, in spite of our tensions and pains, the beauty of being continues to radiate through us with its softening and healing energies.

The realization of our imprisonment and narrow-mindedness is often accompanied by feelings of strong compassion. With empathy, love and even amusement, we observe how an automatic smile or a forced seriousness is imprinted in a face passing us by. We notice and wonder why our back is bent, as if it is carrying a heavy load that constantly weighs us down. And, why are we looking anxiously around, as if someone were thinking badly of us or as if it would be threatening to be seen as we really are? And then, at the dinner table, embarrassed, we may catch ourselves revealing our greed while eating, as if we could never get enough; or we become aware of a ridiculous pride that keeps us bolt upright as if in a suit of armor, almost causing us to stop breathing.

The more this lack of freedom touches our hearts, the easier it becomes to understand how artificial and basically unnecessary all of these behavioral patterns are. In growing amazement, we observe each other, with pain and with a smile. We shake our heads and laugh: "Here we are sitting in paradise, and yet we feel and behave as if we are in hell." With this laughter comes a wondrous moment of awakening.

Vibrating bands of shadow and light are running over the trunks of elms by the river pool. Like a fire coming from deep inside that does not burn – raining light.

CONDITIONING

Our personal interpretation of reality is not reality itself. During the silence retreats I am especially aware of how my own personal conditioning, with its family-rooted behavior patterns and value systems, and my cultural background, automatically define the way I perceive and categorize other people's conduct. How blind I am to assume that the others share exactly the same perceptions and experiences! Over and over again, I am surprised to realize the falsity of these assumptions.

It is always fascinating to discover at the end of a silence retreat how a specific interaction, which occurred during the retreat, was seen and interpreted by five different people in five different ways. When we begin talking again after the period of silence is over, it is amusing to hear the various intricate fantasies and obsessive thoughts we each had in connection with the

event. The common factor in most interpretations is that we each attached a personal and often false meaning to a happening – colored by our own conditioning – which, in reality, had very little or nothing to do with what was actually going on.

THOUGHT COMMENTARIES

I keep observing how thought is constantly commenting upon the actual moment and is, in this way, continuously recreating 'me' in the present. It thinks 'me' to be the one who experiences and senses the actuality of Now. This creates a distancing from the immediate Now and gives it an apparent graspable meaning, obscuring the essential incomprehensibility of each present moment. Once reality is made "graspable", the 'I' can handle it, act in it, and be convinced that – as a separate entity – it is moving inside this unknown presence. As thought, through its very nature, always measures and defines, that which is immeasurable begins to fade away. Its fluidity becomes solidified through ideas, and its transparency transforms into walls. This is of course illusory because, in reality, thought can never touch the transparent.

From where does thought take its hypnotic power to persistently present its constructed worlds and ideas as the one and only reality? Could this be an intrinsic quality which is rooted in the very nature of thought itself? In exploring this phenomenon closely, I observe that thought's hypnotic effect is the inevitable outcome of inattention. As long as thought is not recognized as being merely a thought – and not an independently existing fact – its creations will always present themselves as alive and real. A switch of planes in consciousness goes unnoticed. The transition from simply being to the land of the described is unseen. It requires an enormous degree of alert attention to become aware of this qualitative shift in consciousness at the very moment in which it is happening.

High up, on the topmost branches of the tall trees, the leaves flutter like prayer flags in the wind. They seem joyous and drunken from the light.

While I am sitting on a small stone wall having breakfast, a tiny, light brown caterpillar crawls over the stone slabs on the ground. It is covered with a thousand fine hairs, glistening in the morning sun. Its movement is pure flowing. It will live only a few more days and then be transformed into a moth.

LIGHT-REFLECTIONS

Rays of light, descending through the high trees above me, are reflected on the surface of the quiet water and shine upon the leaves of small bushes next to the river. Water skippers, with their twitchy movements, create tiny circular ripples, causing the reflections on the leaves to vibrate with a fine flickering of light. While the small acorn leaves tremble in the wind, the flickering light brushes their underside and reflects in my eyes. Thoughts quiet down and vision becomes hazy. The flickering fills the consciousness. All becomes blurred.

Today my head feels like it's in a void. The mind is too tired to think. Everything floats undefined in a space of awareness. Nothing is fixed and the hot sun glows.

Now I know why the silence is so different today. The crickets have stopped their singing. It is hard to believe, this absence of sound. For weeks they lent rhythm to the stillness; but today their music has ceased throughout the valley. It seems as if the silence is missing some part of itself.

The yellow is fading
from the fallen leaves.
They themselves
will soon wither,
into dust.

After dinner, huge cumulus clouds build up in the east, their color turned to rosy gold by the setting sun as it vanishes behind the hills. Above them, a white towering cloud is rising ever higher. As darkness settles, the cicadas begin to sing.

THE GROUP IN SILENCE

UPON ARRIVAL

New people have arrived. The house welcomes them with a cosy atmosphere and with fresh flowers in each room, inviting the newcomers to feel at home. The following afternoon, all talking stops.

Each group is a being of its own, slowly forming and developing a particular dynamic and balance. It is like a bouquet of flowers in which each individual flower is unique and special, creating together a distinctive whole. Without words, nearly all participants get along with one another. Freed from the need to agree on arbitrary opinions, it becomes easier to find resonance.

From the very beginning of the retreat, as though in a state of anticipation, there is a noticeable stillness in this group. Or is it that the place itself is so filled with silence that it is contagious?

THE WALKING MEDITATION

The morning is fresh and new. During the walking meditation, raindrops are glistening all over the meadow. It is as if spring sends greetings from afar with blue and white flowers swaying above the previously dry and withering grass.

Standing in a wide circle on the meadow in front of the house, we form an organic whole amid the flowers and tall grass, looking at each other as though for the first time. The walking is slow and the movements flow softly. When all weight is given to one foot, one can feel how the vertical axis between the sky and the earth transmits strength and balance. Step by step, the body glides along. It is still cool and the rising sun opens the pores with its warmth. Everything wakes up.

IN BEING TOGETHER

Quietness and serenity is settling upon the group. Slowly, with time, each one of us becomes more and more visible. Unaccustomed to simply being who and how we are, we first need to develop trust before we can show our true selves to one another – sensing, all along, that only in this way can we reveal our beauty.

Shooting stars
in the sky above.
Like children
we play around
in the kitchen.
The night is laughing.

Every so often, with the setting sun, a unique quietude settles on us at the end of our communal dinners. It spreads through the group like a soft blessing, but it is not of our creation. All at once, with subtle lightness, all is immersed in a space that feels like "being home".

DISTURBANCE IN THE AIR

As the days of silence move on, a state of deep relaxation and tranquillity evolves. And yet, while the body is more sensitive and our perceptions are increasingly refined, it can happen that the brain becomes more vulnerable and inclined to irritability. As subliminal and often insignificant disturbances build up subconsciously, they may surface unexpectedly, causing us to lose that feeling of openness and peace that we had before and launching us into a state of tense confusion.

Looking at this phenomenon, I observe closely the process in which feelings of resentment and anger arise in me. The moment disturbing information enters the brain – for example, when someone approaches me with an uncanny glance or a strange gesture – it is instantaneously interpreted, as a projection that something troubling or disregardful has just been done to 'me'. Or, alternatively, I may assume that I myself have done something wrong. Immediately, my ego-system reacts, often unconsciously, producing unpleasant feelings and physical sensations, reacting as if my self-image had been hurt or attacked. From here on, new waves of thoughts and emotions automatically develop. They boil up and start seething until they occupy the whole space of consciousness with justifications, accusations and tensions. It feels like poison is spreading in a pond. Thought-circles churn up the water, bringing it gradually to the boil. Everything calls for relief through action.

Since such an eruption of emotion is hardly possible in a silence retreat, I can do nothing other than watch and observe this turbulent movement inside of me. It continues to boil until, eventually, the pressure is diminished. The anger or hurt becomes diluted and is finally dissolved. This entire inner episode can unfold within a couple of minutes or last up to several hours. Afterwards, as I look back and recall the whole scenario, I feel astonished and often amused at myself.

With many subtle, energetic communications taking place among the silent participants during a retreat, the group develops into a single sensing organism. As a result, atmospheric disturbances can be felt more or less consciously by almost everyone. As these energetic vibrations spread amongst us, an increasingly strange mood may permeate the space, leading from one irritation to another. We know such similar shifts of mood from our daily lives, where they evolve and spread mostly on an unconscious level. Here, however, in silence, we have the possibility to observe and follow our mood swings clearly and follow their rippling effects on our emotional merry-go-rounds.

Once the dynamics of these movements are understood, it becomes possible to step outside them. Without any further commenting and labelling, the brain can let go and reconnect with the silence. As the disturbance dissolves, peace reappears. Observing how these mood swings drift in waves through the group, I wonder if they are not also drifting throughout the whole human world.

Typically, disturbances and annoyances only develop into serious problems when the thought processes become overly obsessed with them. The mind then concentrates on analyzing, commenting on and interpreting the situation – and the underlying conflict – with the intention of understanding, changing and solving it. While these reactive thought processes are rotating, the conscious space they occupy gets progressively narrower. Occasionally, one can be dominated by such obsessions for days on end, caught inside a mind-based cage built of arbitrary meanings and fixed ideas, to which one attaches utter importance. All direct contact with the present is then blocked off, and the sense of presence completely disappears. Blindly, we circle around ourselves and are no longer there. On rare occasions, which are unlikely to occur during a silence retreat, this state of confusion can evolve to such a degree that delusions start to possess the mind, causing panic and a fear of no escape.

We do not have to go to such extremes in order to understand the basic dynamics of negative mood and behavioral changes. We can become aware of our mental disturbances at a much earlier stage and thus avoid becoming trapped. This can happen the moment we are touched by something real and alive like a deep breath, a flower, the reflection of light, or the warm glance of a human being passing by. It is then that we wake up, filled with relief and amazement.

The storm comes closer.
Sitting in quiet,
we listen together.

Such joy
with the first drops!
Such marvel!
Fresh coolness
caressing the skin.

LAUGHTER

The atmosphere is full of joy today. Everywhere and without reason we greet each other with an amazing smile. Thoughts cannot be taken seriously. During dinner, a young man suddenly starts laughing. Nobody knows why, but it is contagious. He cannot hold it back and his whole body is shaking. Just from seeing it, more and more of us join in, until waves of laughter circle around the table for more than five minutes. Then once again, there is silence.

Laughter is so healthy and healing! In a moment of utter surprise, what at first appeared to be serious breaks down and becomes irresistibly funny. What seemed to be solid and definite is now revealed to be an illusion or an absurdity. This sudden switch of reality triggers contagious laughter in all of us. In spite of having felt separated from one another only moments before, we are now suddenly united, laughing with eyes that recognize one another as if for the first time.

A DAY OF SLOW MOTION

Today even the gong sounds measured while it is slowly carried around the stone house calling us to meditation. All follow the call in slow motion.

Already, during this morning's walking meditation, I anticipate the depth of today's silence. The meadow is breathing with the freshness and innocence of spring, with its many-colored flowers and the glistening dew on the leaves. In front of the mill-house, we walk in a circle to the song of early morning birds, each in his or her own unique rhythm. The soft grass gives way beneath the naked feet, as their supple movements create the impression of a floating gait. While we are all inwardly focussed our togetherness is, nevertheless, clearly to be felt.

Later on, the sound of the gong resonates through the valley once more. As we move in gliding slow motion to the meditation place the world around us seems to transform, becoming almost unreal, and at the same time, extremely intense. A narrow path leads us to an area on the edge of the creek. Here, too, an ungraspable presence pervades the space. Deep stillness calls our attention and brings a peaceful calmness to the mind. All wanting is silenced by the soft touch of the warm breeze.

At noon, in the kitchen, it is time for lunch. We all concentrate on pre-paring our own meals, with our actions performed in slow motion. A young woman carries some vegetables up the staircase. Another carries a plate of cheese in her hands, taking all the time in the world. In a corner of the kitchen a man is sitting, absorbed in watching. What might he see? The milk arrives and leaves again. People are coming and going. Dishes are filled, emptied, washed and dried. For the third time, the cheese is brought back to the refrigerator, while the dishwashing continues in the old stone sink. Everything happens exceptionally slowly and without any noise. Everything is occurring without much intention – as if by magic.

Two and a half hours later, the gong's slow beat sounds like music. All senses are awakened. While walking to meditation, I look towards the forest on my right. Here, too, I am touched by a surprising enchantment; as if in a spell, I see the oaks with their twining ivy and the green blades of grass be-neath them for the very first time. Then, as I step from the full sunshine into the shadow, everything changes again. The brain bathes in freshness and opens up to the new.

At our meditation place the song of the river comes closer and a pulsat-ing shimmer meets the eyes. Here, too, and all around, there is this unique silence. The otherness is everywhere.

During the afternoon meditation nothing exceptional occurs. Every so often I enter a state of simply being, where the 'me' does not really exist … and then again the 'I' re-emerges inside the stories and fleeting films that run through the mind, appearing and reappearing, coming and going.

Later in the day, as my brain begins to feel fatigue from so much atten-tiveness, I look for a place to rest. The slow pace of my movements is still quite natural and in tune with all that is happening around me. I sit down somewhere and suddenly … there is only perception. Everything happens by itself – insects, humans, a dog passing by.

In the evening, everyone gathers peacefully around the eating-place where dinner will soon be served. The sun is gently descending behind the hills in a soft glow of orange and red. No wind. One woman sits with her eyes closed, simply listening. Others, too, appear to be completely absorbed. There is nothing to be done and nobody is doing anything.

During dinner, the movements begin to accelerate. Still, each bite, each taste, is fully enjoyed. Eyes and hands are talking to each other and laughter is in the air. Then, during evening meditation, the immense intensity is there again. The atmosphere of dusk sets in and the birds slowly cease to sing.

Slow motion is not only a matter of voluntarily moving slowly. Doing that would be merely acting. The real secret of moving in slow motion is revealed when one relaxes into slowness. It becomes even more mysterious when one gradually becomes slowness itself and finally disappears in it. Then the movements move in a space of quietness and time stands still. One is closer than ever to experiencing the ongoing reality of creation – and creation is all that is.

What do we sense when we pass each other quietly in slow motion? Two bodies, two movements, two beings. The immediate presence intensifies and we can feel directly the vitality emanating from the other body. An actual energetic exchange takes place between us, a real communication that is not tainted by our thoughts. The pure state of being comes face to face with itself.

Parallel to, and yet quite independently of these energetic encounters, a process of recognizing the other as a defined person is, nevertheless, still continuing to take place. It is a mental activity based upon interpreting the perceived impressions through memory and thinking. Understanding, however, that the genuineness of meetings between human beings does not depend upon recognition, we can begin to experience the immediacy of every encounter without time intervals and mental descriptions. Timeless and nameless, we are instantly together.

For some time, I sit with closed eyes in the kitchen. All noises and sounds appear to be happening by themselves and are no longer connected to the activity of any identifiable person. Additional stories about the others tail off, and I seem to be listening to a kitchen orchestra, playing by itself.

EXPERIENCING THE BREATH

The breath is our constant companion in silence. It is our anchor, connecting us directly to life. It is, therefore, always something special to give and receive breath-treatments, a gentle form of individual bodywork, during a group silence retreat. I feel the preciousness, fragility and the hurting in us humans so intensely during these treatments that, at times, I have difficulties dealing with them. What helps me most is to connect with my own natural breath. It brings calmness and spaciousness into the brain, allowing these qualities to flow through my hands as they touch the other person. In unique moments during a session it may happen that we meet each other directly within the

breath, entering together into oneness. A deepening trust grows that the stream of breath is holding and nourishing us.

Praying hands.
What shall I do?
Wounded we are;
only crusts protect us.
While underneath,
all the pain
that we cause together
to one another.

So much rage,
so much fear,
so much deep sorrow.
The hands are praying.
They plead to the heart
to open itself –
to the light.

Whilst receiving a breath-treatment myself, I slowly calm down and let go, allowing whatever happens to happen. Through the energy transmitted by the treating hands, and their dialogue with my flowing breath, the whole body awareness transforms into a limitless stream of sensations. All feelings of personal boundaries are gone and a surprising experience unfolds: the universe, in its infinity, no longer seems to end at the skin, but, rather, it seems to permeate the whole body. All bones and organs, all cells and con-

necting tissues are in the middle of this cosmic immensity, intermingled with it. The body does not only seem to be inside the universe, but, as well, to consist of the universe. It feels as though cosmic space is penetrating and traversing my physical body in a concrete and material manner. The skin is completely porous and permeable. It is indescribably blissful.

Tasting the grandeur of this experience, even my breath is startled, as if it needs to retreat for a moment in the face of such connectedness.

Relief.
This burdened body lets go.
What a joy, to breathe!
The expanse in between the solid.
The space, that is holding us.
Even the bones are breathing,
they breathe the light.

Unexpected as always,
it is streaming in,
the primordial power. –
All is possible.

INTER-CONNECTEDNESS

During the early morning walk I am spontaneously filled with a strong sense of being connected to all there is – flooded with the sense of a complete and total harmony which does not exclude anything. Everything has its place. Everything belongs together. Everything affects everything else.

Reflecting upon this experience, I wonder which phenomenon existing in our daily lives mirrors this inter-connectedness. To my own surprise the Internet comes to mind, this global "network-in-between". The name itself indicates the fact of being inter-linked. It is an amazing development, representing, as I see it, a huge step in human evolution and the evolution of consciousness.

With this vast computer network it becomes evident that all human knowledge is one singular whole and is equally available to all people. It enables each one of us to communicate and to become, somehow, visible to the rest of mankind, conducting exchanges with each other through internet forums, chat groups, blogs, YouTube clips and a constantly growing variety of internet communities and social networks. Our personal stories are rapidly mixed and shared as we communicate with each other, all day long, all around the globe. The unity of our human consciousness, at least in the areas of knowledge and verbal or visual exchange, has never before been so evident and undeniable.

Knowledge does not belong to anybody; it is the knowledge of mankind. Since knowledge originates from the same source, it is shared equally by all of us, regardless of the fact that each one of us only seems to be in possession of certain parts of it. The Internet and its sibling, the television, the equally influential communal information and entertainment tool, are ceaselessly contributing to the development of a new common culture of humanity. It appears now that the inter-connectedness between all living entities seems to manifest itself in a technological form. Even if it may only be on a superficial level, this developing world of information technology enables every one of us to become aware of our ultimate unity.

While billions of people simultaneously watch an event on TV – for example, the opening of the Olympic Games – or surf by themselves for hours on the worldwide web, a new harmonious synchronicity in consciousness may be evolving whose consequences are still to be known. As alienating as these technical media may seem to be, and as much as they support our addictive drives, they could become the vehicles which may finally bring us together.

MEDITATIVE TALKS

During some of the retreats, we periodically meet for meditative dialogues conducted in a sensitive and contemplative atmosphere. Being grounded in silence, these talks arise from a deep state of listening. All that is present is perceptible inside and in between the words – the murmurs and sounds around, the house with its solid stones, the endless sky and, above all, the presence of each and every one of us. Everything around us affects us directly and changes the weight and impact of our words. The silence – before and after – gives rise to an attentive and receptive way of speaking with each other that we otherwise do not know or practice.

The woven fabric of the spoken words floats alongside everything else that is in the space. The words become discernable. They find resonance, and only then do they elicit a reaction or response. The remarks which follow fall like drops into a lake of awareness, at times without an obvious relation to what was previously said – yet always in harmony with what has been and with what is.

Discussions about opinions regarding what is right and wrong never occur during these talks. The dialogues hold a space where every word and every expression has its place, coming and going like the wind and the heat of the day. As everyone talks authentically from a profound space inside oneself, the most precious part of us becomes visible, the part that we usually hide from each other through words. These periodic talks, interlaced within the days of silence, cause no interruption to the silence. On the contrary, they are an additional vibration which we create together – a vibration that nearly always opens the heart.

After the communal evening meditation, the full moon rises with its yellow-orange glow in the dip between the two hills in the east. Enchanted, we watch with fascination. It touches something deep inside of us, as if the moon is the sister of our soul.

LAST DAY OF SILENCE

Today is the last day of silence with this group. In the hazy heat of the day a strange wistfulness lies over the house and mingles with the odd pre-autumnal feel of something drawing to an end. Once again it has become very still.

Everyone withdraws inwardly. A mood of parting is in the air; and just now, the gong.

Before the last walking meditation, we all stand evenly dispersed around the meadow, like pearls in a circle. As we begin to move together, each one finding his or her appropriate pace, we hear the piercing sound of a power mower coming from the neighbor's house on the other side of the river, reminding us of the outside world. The noise eats into the brain. Amazingly enough I stay calm. When it stops for a few minutes the stillness invades us as rarely before.

Later in the day, autumn storms – a flavor of departure. Heaviness hangs in the air and also inside the heart. The time for saying good-bye comes closer. The focus and density of the atmosphere have changed. One feels that everyone is here and elsewhere at the same time, concerned with his or her particular thoughts. One's daily life is approaching; the difference between there and here is tangible.

Before the first talk.
Raking the ground of the meeting place.
Traces on the wet earth.
Purity of the new.

FIRST TALKING CIRCLE

After the many days of silence, the first sharing circle is always something special. Each person begins with a few soft-sounding words, rings the singing bowl and passes it on. The first round is marked by deep feelings of being moved, of gratitude and of speechlessness. Most of us are like innocent stammering children, and many eyes are moist. There is a great beauty in revealing and seeing the marvelling and unwounded beings within us adults who are so deeply marked by life.

First words tremble in the space. How to express the unspeakable, that which has been so deeply felt inside each one of us? The words are simple and pure. They move us. And, sometimes, they are carried away by the wind, unheard. In the sound and texture of their voices, each one of us is palpable in his and her beauty, like the flowers standing in a glass bowl in the middle of the circle. Such words are like a treasure and it only needs a few. It is enough simply to listen; there is no need to reply.

Dawn sets in.
The swallows are dancing.
Gratitude spreads
inside our hearts.

THE SENSE OF 'ME'

What is it that gives us such conviction and such a secure sense of being a 'me'? What are the roots of the 'I' that constantly nourish it, giving it the appearance of being continuous and undoubtedly real? Like a red thread running throughout the retreats, this question emerges over and over again, and at times, insights come forth which cast some light upon this basic inquiry.

THE BODY

Whenever I ask the question: "Who is the 'I'?" the body comes immediately to mind. The strongest proof for 'my' existence is based upon the unquestioned belief that this body is 'my' body. From early childhood onward, I regard it as a distinct entity belonging inherently to me and only to me; I being the one who feels it and controls it. We all hold on to this innate and unequivocal conviction which is almost impossible to challenge.

Yet, if we examine in detail the intricate subject of the body, we will see that regardless of this sense of ownership of and having control over it, nearly all neurophysiologic and biochemical processes – such as blood circulation, the digestive system or cell metabolism – are involuntary. They happen unconsciously and naturally, without any will or decision on our part. At most, we may use our will to initiate some of our bodily activities. But even then, as with the case of voluntary movements, is it not the body's innate intelligence, rather than the 'I' that guides the coordination and fine – tuning of each of our physical movements? In beautiful and wondrous ways we can experience this while making love. Or, when we consciously learn certain movement patterns, for example in a dance choreography or a Tai Chi form, do we not still have to rely on the body's inner wisdom to perform them?

Our belief that the body exists as a solid, separate and clearly defined entity in the environment comes into question when we begin to analyze the activity of breathing. The air, as a mixture of many components, is blown to us by the wind from anywhere in the world. When I inhale, this air flows with all its different particles into the lungs. It delivers its elements to the blood which distributes them throughout the body and into every single cell. In reverse order, those elements that were previously parts of the individual cells now enter the air and the wind with each exhalation.

Similar processes happen via the skin, through food digestion and excretion. The body is in a constant metabolic process of destruction and reconstruction. Up to ninety percent of all atoms in the body are exchanged every year. Our physical structure is in a complex, continuous and interactive flow with our environment and therefore lives in direct substantial connection with the whole world. When can a body part or particle be called 'mine' and when does it belong to the 'world'?

In spite of knowing all of this, we still experience the sensations and feelings in the body to be completely and personally 'ours'. When there is pain and tension, it is 'my' pain, 'my' tension. And it is the same with pleasurable sensations. We naturally say: "Today, I am in so much pain", or "I feel so relaxed". Never once would we consider these sensations to be non-personal, natural processes which happen by themselves as an expression of many interrelated elements of the holistic movement of life.

In further examining the subject of the body, we find clear correlations between thoughts and bodily sensations which contribute strongly to our sense of ownership of 'our' body. When I have a pleasurable or a fearful fantasy, the body reacts immediately with corresponding sensations. In fact, all intense images stimulate accompanying physical sensations. A good example of this can be experienced in autogenic training, where guided imagery produces feelings of warmth, heaviness or relaxation in the body. This linkage between psychological and physical processes is also reflected in the multitude of so-called psychosomatic illnesses, where stress and mental suffering lead to physical ailments. The psyche and the body seem, therefore, to be completely interconnected and inseparable. When I then ask the question: "Is this really *my* body?" I have consequently also to ask: "Is this really *my* psyche?"

The identification of the 'I' with the body is deeply engraved in us. Since birth, we are taught that this is 'our' body, and from there on, thought continues to describe it as such: as a separate whole, an entity in itself which 'I' inhabit. Yet, this concept of the body is based on thinking and not on sensing. It is only when we observe the body with the eyes that it appears to be a unified form with clear boundaries. The moment we close our eyes, the experience of what the body is transforms significantly.

With eyes closed, the body is practically indefinable – consisting of many different qualities and sensations which are quite separate and independent from each other and which appear to intermingle perpetually with other sensory input. If, for a moment, you observe with eyes closed the stimuli arriving both from the external environment and from within the body, you may experience that there is no basic qualitative difference between physical sensations and other perceptual impressions such as a fragrance, a gust of wind or the sound of running water. When I hear the song of a blackbird or smell from afar the blossoms of a lime tree, those impressions appear to be just as personal and close to me as a pain in 'my' foot or a pleasant feeling in 'my' belly. Though each input is different and unique, none belongs more to 'me' than any other. On this level of awareness, all perceptions blend together into the overall sense of being present. Within this lively assortment of impressions, the body is no longer recognized as a separate entity and, therefore, does not belong to anyone. 'My body' is a mere image of thought.

WANTING AND LISTENING

The path of silence leads us from wanting to listening; the passage into being. Whenever we desire something, our wanting has a direction and we become fixated on an idea – on something that is not actual. It is a movement from here to there. Listening, on the other hand, is quite different. It calls the attention into what is now and is, therefore, a movement from everywhere to here. The 'I' usually wants; therefore it has to become quiet for listening to occur. Only then can the 'I' enter into the vibration from which it is born.

Today again,
a glistening light.
A clearness,
sharp and soft at once.

All wants to burst
out of its form;
reaching out
to the open space.

Then, from nowhere,
a roaring storm,
chases away
the remaining veils.

And now, afresh,
the deepest silence,
pervades the valley
with all its might.

So intensely dense
that the armour breaks.
The heart is uncovered,
bathing in light.

RELATIONSHIPS

Through being with others I become who I am. Our relationships form and determine deeply the sense of 'me' that each of us holds and, therefore, constitute another major pillar of our identity. From birth onwards we live in an ongoing and evolving network of relationships: with our parents and siblings, our partners, children and friends, in our workplace and in our social environment. The closer and more intimate the relationship is, the more it confirms the 'me' as a known and stable reality. In this process the conscious 'I'-image is gradually shaped through language, through what others – especially in the early relationships – communicate to me. Were I to grow up without the human language, as for instance among animals, the sense of 'me' would undoubtedly be different. Whenever I am approached with: "You are …", "You should …", "Why did you …?" I am being seen as, and called into an unquestioned identity; and I am confronted with the self-evident expectation to answer and to react as this identity. Each meeting of this kind tells me: "This is you, the 'you' who I know, the 'you' that you know."

To give an example: only after the death of my mother did I realize how I was still living with the feeling of being a "son" who was shaped through all of our shared memories, and how much the relationship to my mother had formed my self-image. When she died, I primarily felt the loss by no longer having a counterpart to this part of my identity; as if a part of 'me', namely the "son", had also died.

Because of these unconscious and habitual communication patterns in our intimate relationships, we repeatedly invite one another to assume a particular self-image which belongs to that specific relationship – like being a wife, a father or a business-partner. In this way we encourage each other to further decorate and stabilize these images with an array of new stories and labels. This identification with specific roles often prevents us from being able to see each other for who we really are in that particular moment. Consequently, we end up conversing with the person we know from our imagination, rather than the one who stands right in front of us.

When we focus our attention on this phenomenon, we will be surprised to realize how strong this habit is and how much it fortifies and secures our sense of 'me'. At the same time, this very awareness helps us recognize the 'you' and the 'I' as fleeting and transforming appearances. This understanding alone can essentially alter the basis of our relationships. When we now

meet and look at each other, we not only see somebody known in front of us, but become simultaneously aware of facing someone new and unknown. Now the directness of the moment shines in the intimate space between us.

Sometimes unreal,
this mythical light.
Where all commencing sound
drowns.

MANKIND

One could imagine the whole of humanity as a huge organic creature with billions of blossoms and billions of faces. Each face grows out of the whole and is, therefore, an expression of the whole. The child originates from the parents, the parents from the grandparents and the grandparents from the great grandparents, all springing forth from the roots of the tree of mankind. Like the buds that develop into the unique and precise blossoms that they are, our diverse genetic dispositions and different environmental influences evolve and form us into the varied expressions which make up the human race. Our communities and cultures, like the many different branches of the same tree, can be seen as the evolutionary outcome of this entire creative activity which forms humanity.

Essentially, we humans all share the same brain, a brain which has been evolving slowly through the natural unfolding of life. No one of us is an isolated or independent being. On the contrary, we are forever acting in unison, even when we kill each other. We are all parts of smaller or bigger systems in which we assume changing and usually pre-defined roles: in our families, our workplace, our religious communities or our nations. All these systems, with their specific constellations, are interrelated and function as one common whole.

Is it not an absurd notion to think that I could lead 'my' life in an independent state of freedom, just by and for myself? How can we assume that we actually exist as autonomous, self-determining and separate individuals, when in fact, we all belong together to the one big tree of mankind? Together we are lived by life; together, we *are* life.

TIME AND 'ME'

Looking at the stream's running waters and at the passing clouds far above, I feel the days slipping away in the eternity of this very moment. The question arises: "What is time, which seems to fly so fast and yet, all at once, appears to be standing still?"

Time is such a substantial element in our apparent reality, in 'my' reality! My whole sense of identity is based on the belief that I am someone who exists continuously whilst time elapses. Believing that I have been living in time as basically the same person from early childhood to this very day, I say with certainty: "This was my life." Past, present and future are the measures of my self-descriptions, plans, worries and wishes. Without time, I cannot conceive of myself as a continuous 'I'. My belief in personal change and achievement is based entirely on the concept of personal continuity. What an essential conviction this is for all of us! Our whole life is more or less founded upon it. If the future would suddenly disappear as an option, the 'I' would fall into an abyss.

However, is time not a concept of thought with which it measures and arranges the perceived and the imagined? It is a sensible and obviously indispensable tool in the areas of science and technology, in the description of biological and evolutionary processes and in coordinating all of our daily schedules. None of this would be possible without the concept of time. Can we go so far as to conclude that everything which needs thought also needs time?

Do I also need time? Am I made up of time? Will I, the one who is experiencing this very moment, exist tomorrow or in a year or even in the next moment? Do I have continuity in time?

Thought hesitates. It understands that it cannot answer these questions. It needs time; it is *of* time, and therefore all its possible answers carry within them the flavor of time. The 'I' of time, the 'I' of my life-story, is born and arises from thought.

Evening sun after the rain.
Clear and soft its soothing light.
Calming clouds, like feathers white,
are gliding through the light-blue skies.

A buzzard circles far above,
a messenger from far beyond.
Time stands still.
The soul can rest.
A wave of peace
streams through the mind.

LIFE IS HAPPENING BY ITSELF

THE UNPREDICTABLE

In the leisure of a simple daily rhythm free of any external obligations, the days of silence move on and a deep truth gradually begins to reveal itself: life is happening by itself and through itself. Life is acting out itself. In spite of all our plans, control mechanisms and time-structures, every moment is unpredictable and the precise course of any future event is unknown – a sudden blast of wind, an abrupt cry; unexpectedly a heron flies by.

At this very moment, a woman appears from around the house and looks at me. Her gestures prompt me to get up. I am looking for tweezers to pull a thorn out of her foot when, all at once, I hear the noise of the car that brings our food supplies. I help to carry them into the pantry. A delicious-looking peach catches my attention. I take it and leave the room. Opposite the door, I see hundreds of butterflies and insects hovering over the lavender. I sit down and observe them while eating the peach. I look at the clock. One hour is left until the next meditation. "What could I do?" I could write something. Walking to my room, I encounter somebody else. He hands me a book of poetry. I stop, open it and read some lines. From afar, sounds of laughter, and in-between, a subtle poem resonates within me.

Later on, in a sitting meditation, I observe the breath and the stream of thoughts. One cannot predict which thought will come next to mind; one cannot predict what bird will sing which tune next or when and where some nagging pain will be felt in the body. It is all unpredictable. Everything happens by itself, one thing from the other, one after the other. It seems we determine what is taking place inside of us and around of us. However, in reality, it happens to us and we happen as it.

As we delve deeper into this enquiry, it becomes ever more magical and impalpable. There are infinite movements, all occurring simultaneously: the grass, the insects, the trees, the water, the birds, the clouds, we humans and our thoughts, the body, the planets and the galaxies. Countless movements and phenomena occur simultaneously without disturbing one another. Some seem to be self-initiating. Others seem to trigger one other. All appear from nowhere and pass away into nowhere – an incessant coming and going, a ceaseless being born and dying.

I am deeply touched by the permanent transience surrounding me, and by the impossibility of holding on to anything. Observing the perpetual changes in our bodies we recognize, of course, that we are growing older. What is unfamiliar to us is the direct realization that all changes are taking place in the *Now*. It is now that everything dies and now that everything comes newly into being. What a miracle is creation that it should constantly regenerate itself! How wondrous it is, gazing into the infinite night, into this vast space, filled with countless stars and such profound stillness!

Behind all the "whys"
there is One.
Open the questions.
Allow them to be drawn
to the bottom
of this mysterious lake.
Like drops in the water,
there,
they dissolve.

Like captive balloons, we sail through the world, floating past each other, greeting one another with waving hands. In the balloon's basket we carry all that we own and all that we are. Should we allow everything to fall away, we would rise up into the immeasurable.

ABSORPTION

For hours I sit by the water, gazing into its reflections. It arouses such fascination in me; as if only in the reflected does everything become clear. In the depth of the water, the skies become even wider and shades of light blue mingle with dark green. From the surface of this mirror, the trees shoot up trembling, and the three-dimensional opens into an additional realm; it is as if all reflections are just a dream and, in between, shines the real.
After yesterday's heat, today the gentle warmth of a late summer day. A blessing! At the meditation place there reigns such quiet that from far away, even the sound of the creek is heard once again. It is not a murmur – this word is already too loud. It is like a hint of a sound which the hum of a passing fly can drown. All senses are open as this mysterious tone lures us into stillness, into the space between the waves – there, where the breath is born. Then comes the wind. And in its unique way, as always, it carries everything away, bringing back freshness and joy.

A sacred day.
All is blessed.
A sparkling droplet
reflects your face.

CONTEMPLATION OF EVIL

For quite a time I kept my eyes closed, observing inner films, feelings and sensations floating by. At one point images from the war in Iraq emerged – terrible images. Memories of my deep indignation about this war became vivid, leading me to the emotionally-charged question: "How can we understand and how can we deal with all the atrocities, the brutality and recklessness that we humans so often inflict upon each other? How should we deal with the 'evil' in the world?"

Sitting and listening to this question for long periods of time, I did not allow my mind to stray off into ideological or intellectual concepts. Instead, an uninterrupted sensing and probing into inner spaces was triggered by the question. Many sensations, emotions, images and thoughts surfaced and passed through. Slowly, some hesitant insights appeared and soon dissolved again. The whole question seemed to be such a puzzle. If we are all one, if we are all born from the same source, why do we kill, torture and suppress each other?

I found myself unexpectedly flooded by a deep feeling of compassion for us human beings and for the immense blindness, ignorance and insensitivity that enables us to commit all these horrifying deeds. At the same time, I felt as if my intellect was hitting a brick wall, unable to find a valid answer to the question of how to deal with "evil".

Apparently the "bad" does exist. Apparently, it is an undeniable part of our life. It is a fact that we humans have to acknowledge, in ourselves and everywhere around us. Does that imply that we have to accept this without judgment and resistance? Does it mean that we have to develop an attitude of tolerance towards everything, so that we can be at peace even with war? Could it be that moral values, such as "good and bad" or "right and wrong" are altogether inadequate measures that put labels on ungraspable facts, thus creating distance between the actual "evil" phenomena and ourselves so that they do not touch us directly? Is our labelling just like a Band-Aid which attempts to distance us from the "awful" facts and protect us from their naked truth?

If that is so, is it possible that we have to perceive and feel the war images on television, the abuse of children, or the greedy corruption we witness all around us with the same openness with which we witness "beautiful" phenomena – phenomena such as a meal lovingly prepared for the poor or a walk on a radiant snowfield high in the mountains?

Is it possible that "good" and "bad" forces simply exist in the creative cosmos, to be acted out according to their nature, in the same way as forces such as gravity or magnetism? Do all phenomena and occurrences in our world – whether they be horrible or beautiful – originate from the interplay of such forces and their diverse tendencies? Can we look at war and peace not as contradictions, but rather as two sides of the same coin, belonging together just like pleasure and pain?

My mind searches for answers. It goes in circles and ends the quest as it began: deeply moved, full of compassion and without understanding or finding a way out. How should I know? How can I know? It is beyond my grasp!

As I ponder and listen to answers which come and go, one insight becomes clear to me: in spite of all our sufferings and sorrows, we will never be able to escape this state of hostility, contradictions and deep conflicts as long as we are driven by our dualistic mind, fighting with one force against another. As long as we keep on identifying with one of two sides, the fighting, injustice and discrimination will go on forever. Of course, and understandably, we feel a deep inner dismay when confronted with atrocities and terror and predictably react automatically with outrage, defense and attack. Self-righteously, we want to protect ourselves, punish the guilty ones, and engage in "legitimate" counteractions. Yet, the whole history of mankind shows that conflicts, fights and wars were never resolved through polarization, revenge or retaliation, but were instead, continuously prolonged by such reactions. The evening news confirms this day after day.

To develop a fatalistic attitude towards this apparently unavoidable destiny will not free us from our fragmented, dualistic and antagonistic world view. Such an attitude continues to define 'me' as being detached from the events occurring in my life and consolidates yet another illusion: namely, that we are helpless victims in the world of those outer forces and that we are at the mercy of our karma, doomed to tolerate it passively. An illusion of this kind may easily trigger reactions of utter despair and depression.

Liberation from this prison of conflicts and suffering may only begin when we stop intellectualizing, when we drop our ideologies and self-righteous arrogance and become unpretentious and humble, when we bow down and accept our not knowing and our limitations. True liberation is only possible when we realize that there are activities taking place in our human world which are beyond our will and comprehension, and that we have to accept them for what they are without closing our hearts. Then, feelings of compassion can grow and spread, leading us to accept that many appearances and happenings in the world are intangible. They come and go, and we are at the center of them: be it the birth of a baby, the eruption of a volcano, two people making love, cancer in the body, the execution of a man on death row – and even war.

With this understanding, we may allow yet another reality to reveal itself – one that is wholesome and harmonious, that unifies everything and manifests the creative power and intelligence behind all. This highest intelligence is clearly beyond all of us. It pervades and rules the whole cosmos and every living thing, holding all worldly phenomena in its hands. No person alone, no dictator or greedy executive is solely responsible for the suffering and for the cruelties and the evil in the world. They belong to all of us and to the incomprehensible dance of life.

Listen my friend
to your friend.
Inside the stream,
inside the wind,
he is talking to you.

Inside the mountains
and the sea,
his whispers are heard.
Voices and music from afar,
and yet,
their touch so close.

Listen my friend,
yes, listen now.

And soon, with wonder,
you will find,
that inside of all,
this friend is – you.

PLAYFUL PRESENCE

The *only* unquestionable reality is the present moment, with its presence. Every time we exchange glances we are reminded of it. Each gust of wind, each dancing leaf, each simple meal reminds us of it. Each drop of water, each radiant sunset and each breath reminds us of it.

Being together in silence naturally invites us to open up to this presence and to express it through our behavior. Mirrored in the presence, many of our encounters and our related reactions transform themselves into a flowing natural theater on the common stage of life. Nearly everything becomes light and without special significance, often inviting us to laugh. In our movements, we glide through the world and play with each other like children who are rediscovering their innocence. Enacting ourselves in the present, we become more fluid and brighter.

Aware that we are playing together and that all is a dance, we are able to let go of our usual, self-observing, judgemental or insecure selves. Instead, we are like cheerful actors in changing roles whose behavior rarely reflects the serious belief of being somebody important, or of doing something deeply meaningful. Iridescent thought bubbles are dancing in all of us and burst in the wind.

When the purity of being is sensed, its loving vibration naturally enters our play. Where the essence is love, there are only lovers on the stage. And when our eyes meet, they talk the same language, the language of love.

Inevitably, however, this space narrows and lightness disappears. Once again we identify increasingly with our different roles, and with the 'I'. The play becomes serious again. Through defining and evaluating ourselves and our conduct, our personal thoughts and feelings become laden with importance and meaning. We separate and distance ourselves from each other, and the dramas of our lives begin to dominate the content of our minds. Everything solidifies, becoming dense and impenetrable. For us, this transformation in consciousness is always deeply astonishing and even alarming.

If we succeed in such moments to pause, to take a few breaths and observe the situation we are in without evaluation, we can discern the distinct processes of identification with our many attachments and our personal ways of "getting hooked". By pausing, these processes, with their specific energetic qualities and their inherent impulses, become suspended in front of our inner eye. Having lost their potency, they no longer lead us to react immediately or to act out. Often, this is enough to enable us to return to the present moment and to sense again the subtle fragrance of being. Now, we can slowly let go and start to dance again.

We breathe each other
in sun-soaked light.
The flowers and me,
we are one.

In every cell,
in every leaf
life breathes us.

What perfect wonder
holds this form,
what fragrance,
permeates through all!

Early in the morning, everywhere there is mist. When the sun finally rises above the hills, it shines pale through the drifting veils, as if it were arriving late. During the walking meditation, the grass is wet. Here and there, spider webs already stretch between the flowers' stems.

Every morning, we walk our circles around the mill's meadow and each time so much has been transformed. There are always new buds and new blossoms that open, then wither and decay. The colors change. The forms change. Each day there is a new light. We, too, are different, never looking the same. And still, an order remains inside all that comes and goes.

BASIC TRUTHS

All appearances are transient.
The 'I' is imagination.
Only the present exists.

THINKING, FEELING, SENSING

THE INNER CINEMA

For hours I watch my inner movies drift by, while outside, shadows are wandering with the moving sun. The experience of my inner cinema is so fascinating and so alluring that the scenes appear to be actually happening right now. Though the film contents are projected from memory or imagination into my field of awareness, their apparent existence leads to intense emotional reactions and physical sensations which mix with the pleasurable warmth of my skin.

All at once, the blinding sun, shining upon my face through the rustling leaves, interrupts the film, and I become newly aware of my surroundings. In that very moment I understand: Aliveness itself is only *now*! It appears as if the Now breathes life into the movie scenes which run inside the mind, creating the illusion that the content of these scenes are actual alive reality. Yet, they are only images – memories from the past or projections into the future or even pure fantasies. As real as they appear to me, they are not an actual happening. Like the stories in even the best works of fiction our inner films are basically lifeless. Only through the actual aliveness of the perceiving mind do they appear to be alive themselves. Yet only the Now lives! If all images would be erased and the projector would be turned off, nothing of the aliveness of this moment would be lost. The sunlight, the breathing and the presence would still give me the perfect sensation of *being*.

I can clearly observe how the 'I'-image, which is the main actor in these movies, is perpetually charged with a seeming sense of aliveness and realness through the customary habit of automatically replaying, over and over, such emotionally intense inner films. A "breath of life", is, in this way, instilled into our sense of identity. It almost seems as if life wears the costume of 'I' in order to gain awareness of itself.

You,
flower among flowers,
you look upwards
into the sky.
A breeze sets you quivering,
as your leaves tremble
from delight.

You,
being among beings
you unfold today.
Your purple glistens
from the dew,
the nightly kiss
whose gentle touch
awakened you.

You,
vibration in vibrations,
even your bones
are made from light.
Your perfume pervades
as never before,
a gold-dust scent
from hidden worlds.

This morning, a miracle of roses: three wide-open blossoms of Gloria Dei! Upon their soft, pink-yellow petals big and small drops of dew are shining like see-through pearls. In the sun they transform into a sea of multi-colored rainbows. Each glance drinks and breathes them in.

DREAMING

Within our world of dreams, we can continue to watch our personal movies even as we sleep. Our dreams help us to explore and understand our brain's amazing capacity to produce seeming realities. During the dreaming process, all thinking, feeling and sensing systems are working fully and demonstrate a staggering complexity, speed and associative fantasy. While the body is asleep, the brain – or possibly even another source – conjures highly intense worlds that appear to be completely real; one next to the other, one inside the other. From where does all this material come? From where are these unknown figures, contexts and relationships invoked? It is as if a magician were playing with an unlimited repertoire, producing it all out of nothing.

We have the tendency to interpret and give meaning to our dreams, thus adding more meaning to ourselves. Some of us even take our dreams as proof that we do not need a body in order to have an identity which can communicate as a separate entity among other beings. As far as dreams are concerned, this may even be true. Yet, when I wake up in the arms of the morning and take a first step in the fresh grass, what does it matter where I was in my dream?

Awakened in a sudden shudder.
Where is the night?
Am I the dream,
appearing real?
Who is this me?
Where is my world?
Where is the ground
that safely holds?

The blackness' light
is blinding bright.
My gaze has cracked.
I know no more.
I fly and topple,
falling deep.
Falling in,
and falling through,
who knows
where to.

Observing a brownish-patterned butterfly drinking naturally from a water drop on the tip of a blue thistle, I ask myself: "Why do we drop bombs on top of each other?"

A dead worm is lying on a warm stone slate, surrounded by hundreds of tiny reddish ants which are eating him up. Transformation.

HOMAGE TO THOUGHT

Oh thought, you wondrous tool of creation! Like an artiste high up on the flying trapeze, you are capable of almost anything. The human arena is your circus tent where you give birth by magic to what appears so real. You are able to connect each and every thing and out of nothing you make something. A spark suffices for you to create my entire world with just a tiny movement. I dance and fight, I suffer and bathe in pleasure as you permit. You provide me with all that I call mine and can take it away at will.

You are an artist of subtle feelings and a dervish in the land of emotion. You reign over the body with tempting illusions, coming and going as you please. Your influence can be felt even from a distance and all that has ever been thought of is contained within you. Among all of creation's children, you are a special child because you generate division. And yet, you, too, are of the eternal womb. Realizing this with laughter, you let go your magic spell.

Sudden rain,
pouring down from the sky.
The earth breathes deep.
She opens her pores,
drinking it all,
this blessing of water.

Where do the roots of the big wisteria find water in this blazing summer to produce such fresh blossoms in the middle of August? Like a big tree, they must grow inside this rocky earth, searching and sucking without losing heart. Her thick trunk has been growing for years and her trailing branches nearly cover two walls of the stone house. She is hard and ever-twining, and produces grape-shaped flowers of delicate pink. Her vigor is so fierce that we are compelled to tame her, concerned that, otherwise, she will break the walls.

ANXIETY

Sometimes, during the silence, attacks of fear, insecurity and anxiety may flood the body and the mind. They can come from nowhere for no reason. Or, they can be triggered by something actual – by a memory or by projections into the future. Being here in the safe environment of a retreat, with no external obligations, gives us a unique opportunity to closely observe such difficult moments of fear.

Usually we use the word "anxiety" as a label for quite complex physical sensations which we interpret in the mind. They consist of a mixture of physical phenomena such as restlessness, tension, pressure or constriction in the chest and stomach, heart racing, sweating, weakness, paralysis, dizziness and many others. As soon as these physical sensations are felt, thought processes automatically begin to interpret them and to associate and compare them with similar experiences from the past. Thought describes these phenomena as happening to 'me' and as a mental state of 'me'.

In this way, the 'I' identifies entirely with the phenomena happening in the body and anxiously says: "I am so frightened". While thought continues to paint a self-image of the 'me' being in danger, being unsafe or unable to cope with the situation, it races around, looking for reasons for what is happening and frantically searching for possible ways of escape. A feedback loop between thoughts and sensations develops in which they reinforce each other and increase in their intensity and urgency. This process is further accelerated through thought's tendency to project ideas about possible consequences, imagining and fearing all that could happen if the anxiety continues: "If this does not stop, I will faint or I will get a heart attack" or "If I don't leave immediately, I will make a fool of myself or I will go crazy".

The process may also occur the other way around. It can begin with an inner film of projected images and ideas; for example, being anxious about an impending exam or remembering a daunting experience with somebody. These projections ultimately evoke the above-described physical sensations, confirming to us that the thought content is justified and real. The reciprocity between thinking and sensing can culminate in intense experiences, leading to a state of panic in which one's whole system desperately searches for an escape or becomes paralyzed.

In such situations, it is extremely helpful to effectively disassociate the thought processes from the physical sensations, so that thought ceases to describe and interpret the sensations and to create terrifying stories around them. This is not an easy step to take because the whole process happens rapidly and quite automatically. It would be like flipping a switch in the brain which stops those fear-inducing specific thoughts from forming. We will only succeed in doing this when we withdraw attention from all thought projections and shift our focus to something other than thought. It can be especially effective, for example, to direct one's attention to one's breath which is already flowing with our feelings and sensations. Alternatively, one can focus attention upon the actual, unpleasant bodily sensations themselves, uniting with them, yet without calling them by name, simply allowing them to be what they are.

The secret is to allow the commotion to flow, as itself, in consciousness, within its own energy and quality – just a streaming movement of physical sensations. Without any description, interpretation or meaning, they do not belong to anyone. There is no 'me' who has them and wants to get rid of them. They are just happening, exactly as the breath is happening. They are there for as long as they last, and then they dissolve naturally, as does everything else that comes and goes. Like a thunderstorm or an earthquake in awareness, they are a natural happening.

Surfing the wind,
this gentle wave.
From afar arises
its melodious sound.

Taking me in,
lifting me up,
like a father his child.

Soothing my skin,
kissing my face,
it brings pure joy.

A caress of eternity.

PHYSICAL PAIN

Physical pain is such a complex and difficult sensation for all of us! It hurts, it irritates, it makes us uneasy and tense, it lets us suffer and despair, and at its worst, it develops into a tormenting torture. It is, therefore, completely understandable that we try to avoid pain and strive to get rid of it the moment we have it. We will go as far as accepting even the most extreme medical procedure in the hope that it will relieve us from our ongoing pains and psychic suffering.

If during the retreats we observe the phenomenon "pain" more closely, we will see that it consists – as do our anxieties – of two distinctly different elements: the uncomfortable physical sensations themselves, and the corresponding 'me', who experiences these sensations as his or her own, reacts to them and wishes to be rid of them.

For some days I feel a deep nagging ache in my upper spine that hinders me from moving freely. Observing it closely I ask myself: "What is the difference between such a pain and any other physical sensation, like hunger, lust or the wind touching my skin? Why can't I let the pain flow with everything else that is around and inside of me?"

The reason seems to be that such relentless pain is so deeply disturbing that my body, quite independently, constantly tries to find relief through a change of position or movement. I experience these spontaneous reactions as completely natural and necessary. They probably stem from the body's deep-rooted survival instinct.

However, it is relevant for me to notice that, all along, while feeling this natural instinctive impulse in the body, my mind, simultaneously and con-tinuously, talks about 'me' having the pain and being disturbed by it. It starts painting dark pictures about my future and about getting older. It re-bels against the impairment and tells 'me' to pull myself together. It develops a whole film full of self-pity and resentment. Over and over again, the think-ing mind searches for solutions offering relief or settles into a mood of numb-ing resignation.

During all of this, thought is constantly fighting the actual pain treating it like an enemy. Through the ongoing description of my affliction, the atten-tion focuses upon my impaired mobility and upon the mental irritation and disturbance that it evokes. 'My' aches become almost the focal point of my existence, excluding most other impressions from my field of awareness. In much worse situations this typical way of dealing with pain can result in an agony that continuously worsens and the whole condition develops into a severe problem. Though it might, in fact, be a physical problem, it has now become a psychological one as well.

In seeing this, I find it helpful to experiment with different approaches to handling pain. Making a conscious decision, one can withdraw the energy from the storytelling process and with undivided attention delve into the painful sensations themselves. If one completely penetrates the actual physi-cal agitations and remains solely with them, without commenting on them, they often transform. One might have the impression of spaces opening in between the "pain-particles", which then alleviate or even dissipate the un-pleasant sensations. It may feel as though the "pain-particles" oscillate in a subtler and less disturbing way.

Another approach to meeting pain is to consciously breathe together with the hurt feeling how, with each exhalation, a certain relaxation and release become possible. Similarly, using an inner visualization process, one can send a stream of light or healing energy towards the painful area, which can also bring about amazing results. Alternatively, one may focus on other accompanying sense impressions like the sound of the water, the movement of the clouds and the summer heat, thus allowing the pain to fuse together with these newly-felt sensations – letting the water, the warmth, or the space with its light, caress the pain and absorb it.

Through all of this, a feeling of compassion develops towards the ailment, so that it is no longer treated as an enemy, but rather as a sibling who we care for. Instead of pitying 'myself' I allow for a more loving, attentive energy to flow towards the areas that are afflicted. This has an immediate positive effect and, though the pain may not entirely go away, a clear relief can be felt.

As we grow older, I feel it is increasingly important to develop a caring and accepting attitude towards all the ailments and changes the body goes through. To fight these natural processes is an utter waste of energy! It is a battle that can never be won. Pain is such a great teacher! It can teach us humility and show us a road which unifies the pleasurable and the non-pleasurable, a path of non-duality.

I look into the mirror.
A stranger is there.
Who entered this house
which used to be mine?

I am so young,
he is so old.
How come
we suddenly are one?

SEXUAL PLEASURE AND DESIRE

Waves of sexual passion and delight – how much energy and power they contain! This primal passion erases everything else and moves in pulsing vibrations towards pure ecstasy and melting fusion. Hardly anything can stop these intoxicating energies from moving bodies and bringing them to the peak of sexual union. All we want is to intermingle, dissolve in each other and become eternally one. What a wonderful gift this is! It is possibly here that we find it easiest to be at one with our bodily sensations, to surrender completely and leave all thought behind.

Nonetheless, it is often the case, either prior to or following such times of extreme joy, that we might find ourselves in an arena of either sweet or conflicting entanglements or, at times, even deep human affliction. The ego is rarely so exposed, both to itself and to others, as it is in its desire for and its approach to sexual pleasure. Here, the ego can experience its own extremes. The whole movement of desire, which is such a basic force in our lives, can be intensely observed in the realm of erotic attraction. Our tendencies to want, to hold on to, to dream and fantasize, to fight for, to resent, and even to hate and seek revenge, are all present in this arena of life.

As unification is always followed by separation, and as the peaceful fulfillment comes to an end, we can observe over time how our inner images and thoughts constantly create intense films of longing, love and all sorts of romantic and sexual fantasies. If, after some time the relationship sours and conflicts arise, the films become more sentimental, dramatic, even tragic and full of jealousy, with thoughts of revenge and self-pity. It is a real challenge to experience all the beauty and wonder of lovemaking, with its lust, intimate closeness and peaceful togetherness and then, to let go without wanting more. It is difficult to feel intense attraction without falling blindly into the slipstream of desire.

Maybe, when we learn to consciously experience our feelings and sensations of lust, passion and love as embedded in the mystery of all the other wonders in nature and in the infinite space of the cosmos, a new, much deeper dimension can enter our lovemaking. When we feel that we are immersed in and carried by the flowing energies of the living presence, we might naturally become less possessive, and learn to surrender and let go. It is then that we may achieve a real balance in our partnerships and begin to truly love.

This morning,
in radiant sunlight,
the cactus opens
her chalice blossom.
Just one flower,
one each year.

Slender boned
its pointed leaves.
What perfect beauty
in tender pastel!
Its bountiful mouth,
so sensually pure,
a willing surrender
to the bath of light.
Inside are stars
and pink pollen dust.

Tiny the cactus,
just barely noticed,
carrying now
on an endless stalk
this morning's glorious queen.

Already by night,
she closes her lips,
to wither away
on the following day.

BEING HERE

At a certain point on one's path of self-discovery it can become clear that the aim is not to reach a certain "state" of consciousness or to achieve a basic change in oneself. All signposts and methods towards that end become relative. The constant preoccupation with oneself is revealed as a habitual stirring of the mind, an entanglement that makes little sense. How strenuous it is to paint and to sustain all these self-portraits and try to understand their meaning! How much more natural it is to enter into simplicity and into that which is given! Why deal with intellectual constructions concerning spiritual hierarchies and different states of consciousness when, from one moment to the next, life is happening right now? We are blessed with breath and light and all is here. Peace and serenity welcome us in.

Our basic task in life may, therefore, be to learn the art of *being*, rather than to search for something that is not here or strive to become somebody we are not. Such aspirations and drives are based on the yearning to sway the assumed identity of the 'I', from where it is right now, towards another situation such as a state of enlightenment, a romantic affair, or a job promotion. Yet, the envisioned change is in this moment nothing other than an image; a fantasy conjured in our mind.

Numerous books have been recently published on "how to become a happy human being". Many seminars and courses currently offer ways to actualize goal-oriented intentions in daily life and to realize one's personal dreams. A huge, heavily commercialized market of "self-realization-programs" – full of promises – has been designed that may support and help many people, but might end up harming others. The aim is frequently to reprogram and recondition the 'I' in order to change deeply engraved behavior patterns. What these functional approaches invariably miss is basic insight into the complex nature of the 'I' itself and, above all, an emphasis on the immediacy of being with the wonders of life.

When we allow ourselves, occasionally, to completely forsake the wish to be different and to stop our endless searching, then we are simply who and what we are, and that is all. This switch in consciousness is not the outcome of a process of inner resignation or depression. It is inspired by the intuitive insight that only in the Now can something be discovered which is beyond the 'I', something that nourishes our innermost being and is unquestioningly always here. In contact with our true inner being we are right here. We are home. And here, we discover that everything else is also here. Life itself takes us in its arms and we need nothing else.

When I am not in the process of becoming or holding on to something that has passed I am not of time. When I am not of time, I dissolve and melt into the all-pervading state of being: 'I *am*'.

I want to go
nowhere,
I am already there
where I am.

Late at night the Indian tanpuras are playing again – music of the spheres. This cosmic sound-fabric dissolves all and unites all. Spirals of infinite harmonies circle as they rise and fall. The space is transparent, yet holds us while the ether sings. The brain is bathed by caressing waves that bring release. All cells are in resonance. Without questions, we all can surrender.

Liquid sun
in flowing waters.
Transparent ground
of vibrant space.

No-man's land now,
untouched by all.
No grain of dust
from what has passed.
Neither you nor me,
neither eye nor ear
were ever here.
This fragrance stills
the breath itself.

Wordless is all.
Those names make here
no sound nor sense.
Just streaming waters,
water in water,
chanting their songs.

THE PRESENT, THOUGHT, AND THE 'I'

As the inner dialogues quiet down, a new reality opens up which does not originate from thinking. It is a singular flowing whole. It is of itself, itself. Without description, without thought, it is being.

THE BRAIN, THE PROCESS OF THINKING AND THE 'I'

The miraculous human brain, having evolved over millions of years and growing anew in every embryo and every infant is, in its early stages, most probably devoid of any traces or imprints. Only during late pregnancy and after birth does the imprinting process start. It always fills me with awe to imagine the pure beauty of this pristine, malleable brain with its enormous potential and sensitivity.

Following birth, all human brains go through intense processes of inner and outer discovery, in which all perceptions, interactions and encounters create imprints, paving neuronal pathways and circuits which form the foundation of our individual conditioning. Already during these crucial first years, the brain manifests the amazing human capacity to produce images, thoughts and feelings with specific contents and qualities, as well as the capacity to store and memorize them. All brains are equipped with, and therefore share, these same basic functions. Essentially, we are all endowed with the same miraculous brain. Keeping this in mind may help us to feel closer to our neighbors as well as to our enemies.

Thinking, similar to all other organic body processes, is the outcome of a complex neurophysiological activity in the brain and is, therefore, an activity of life itself. For millennia, these organic thought processes have produced representations of perceptions of the body and the outside world. These representations, or reproductions, are amazing creations as they form the basis of our conscious experiences. Though we constantly believe these creations to be the direct perceptions of an "objective" reality they are actually the outcome of intricate and mostly unconscious transformation processes in the brain. They may, therefore, be compared to the shadows in Plato's cave allegory, which the prisoners take to be the only existing reality. And the question arises: "How real is our reality?"

In addition to these representations of actual perceptions, thinking creates abstract linguistic constructs in the form of concepts, projections and ideas. These constructs form the basis of many of our imaginary visions, creative images and infinite ideas, which lead to manifold expression in the arts, in new inventions and in scientific experiments. On the other hand, it is this same capacity of the brain to produce ideas which also provides the material for our endless ideological and opinionated battles.

Lastly, thought processes are also the building blocks of the ego-structure, and are mainly responsible for the emergence of the 'I'-image, the 'me'. One of the main characteristics of this 'I'-structure is that it experiences itself as a separate entity which is actually doing the thinking, perceiving, sensing and feeling. It is an amazing puzzle of human existence: the thought process creates an 'I'-image which is then convinced of creating thought itself. The fact that each one of us is certain of being a self-aware 'me' is the outcome of this process.

In reality, this 'I', and the whole ego-structure consist mainly of thoughts, images, memories and brain imprints, including all their accompanying complex emotions and feelings. Its walls are made of flowing films that are constantly changing, though at times they seem to be standing still. Although the process of film production is an activity of the brain and is, therefore, clearly alive, the film content itself is of a completely different character. It is composed of numerous abstract images and projections whose apparent meaning and significance have probably been developing slowly throughout human evolution and conditioning.

To a certain extent, our so-called "known" world, the world which forms the basis of our self-images, is a conceptual-linguistic construction which must have evolved through time into an agreed-upon human "reality". Since this "reality" comes into being mainly through thinking, it is defined and confined by the specific structures and qualities of thought. Being absorbed by this "reality", we often forget that there is a fundamental difference between these thought-constructions and sensory activities like breathing, listening to music or touching the trunk of a tree in the wind.

After the evening meditation,
looking into the sky, no moon.
Only the vast dome and innumerable stars.
The mighty presence of immensity.

How little we know.
Yet the darkness does not frighten.
Granting safety, shelter and peace
it is the shine of the night
protecting and holding us.

BEING, SENSING, THINKING

This essential difference between "being", "sensing" and "thinking" is rarely taught in our modern upbringing and education because we, as parents and educators, are ourselves not consciously aware of the relevance of these differences. Instead, the thought-interpreted world, with its conventional worldview and its understanding of the 'I', is emphasized in our upbringing and gets automatically transmitted, imprinted and elaborated anew in each individual brain. From birth onwards, our interaction with the environment, in combination with the complex process of education, consolidate this abstracted way of understanding oneself and the world, thus moulding our personal human conditioning. It is the basis for the consensus on which our society is founded and from which it functions.

This consensus, however, overvalues a sense of reality that is created by thinking and neglects the reality that is based upon sensing and connecting with the immediacy of the Now. This might be a reason for the many problems and misunderstandings we face throughout our lives. It might be the price we are paying for having eaten from the tree of knowledge. Yet, the tree of life is always close by. Once we eat from its fruit, the 'I' fades away into the miracle of being.

CONSCIOUS AWARENESS

There is another crucial and complex aspect of thought which is essential to understand. It is thought's unique capacity to see itself in action – to be self-aware. This self-reflective quality allows a conscious perception of the thinking processes and the possibility to observe how the 'I', with its self-image and its convictions, is formed. Such observation implies a completely different quality of thinking. It is an "impersonal" way of thinking which is free of comment, judgement and evaluation and is, therefore, beyond any divisions. Thinking, in this form, is none other than immediate, attentive awareness – seeing without a seer. Perhaps the best description for this capacity of the mind is "conscious awareness" – a way of seeing which reveals the qualities and limitations of thought and knowledge. Because of this all-inclusive capacity of "conscious awareness", the great potential and beauty of thought becomes accessible and can be used as a miraculous tool of creation.

Thinking is a lively, creative activity in the brain, occurring alongside all other phenomena and wonders of life – the murmuring of a stream, the humming of a bee, the shine of the moon reflected in the lake. Together with everything else that is happening, sequences of thoughts flow in consciousness, in the living movement of Now. The actuality of being is not based upon thinking. Thoughts are, therefore, only one aspect of the totality of being. Recognizing its own limitations and relativity, thought naturally calms down and ceases to apply its powers where they are inadequate. Silence reigns and the intelligence of life itself now talks.

All suns grow pale
in the light
of a sun
behind all suns.
The shadows vanish,
the forms shatter.
Dreamless gleams
the void.

PRESENCE AND THE 'I'

Presence is *I am.*
>Now is *I am.*
>*I am* is aliveness.
>*I am* is the sense of being.
>*I am* is presence.

Thought asks: "What is the relationship between the *I am* of the present and 'my I'?"
>In listening carefully to the question, the following insight takes shape:
>'My I' is a thought.
>Presence is being. Presence cannot be thought of. It is.
>'My I' lives its seemingly separate existence within the limitless beingness of the *I am.*
>'My I' cannot touch this vibrant reality of being but becomes visible as one of the many appearances in it.

Most of the time, I live 'my' reality, which is my life-story, inside a capsule, shut off from the immensity of the present. It seems as if 'my' world is composed of a different substance, existing separately from the rest of creation. Then, all at once, by unexpected grace, the veil is lifted and presence touches 'my' consciousness. What happens then?
>As if lifted into another reality, I feel loved and perceive the radiant beauty of the outer and inner worlds. It appears as if airy rays of light are shining through my preoccupations and my "important" problems, causing them to float with ease. Held by the presence, the heart is filled with compassion and gratitude for all that exists. Love and peace are here, providing me with the secure feeling of having finally arrived.
>And still, over and over again, I seem to plunge in a quantum leap from the present moment back into my old, known identity. Immediately, the 'I' returns to dominate with all its habitual mechanisms. Within seconds, an abrupt change in consciousness takes place, and I find myself coming back to 'my' stories, experiencing 'my' self as the solitary initiator and controller of all my actions. Again in this "normal" state of mind, the present is defined by the environment surrounding 'my' body, consisting mainly of separate objects and manifestations that are related to 'me'. As a consequence, the 'I' seems to move 'my' body in the defined landscape of a separate and independently existing world.

How different is this feeling to that of being in the immediate presence of Now! Here, the body and the presence are inseparable – they are an integral whole. In this state, when the entity which we call "the body" is moving, the presence walks within it. The body is not walking; the presence walks. Everything moves together. Without the 'I' and 'my' world, the apparent isolation and separateness of the body disappears. The body is no longer 'mine'. It breathes and moves in a flowing exchange with all.

And once again
from nowhere-land
she touches us.
Reminding me,
reminding her,
that she exists.
Appearing first
like a memory,
a distant dream
that once was real.

Until I sense
this vibrant light,
the streaming breath
of presence now.
Then, all at once,
I clearly see
that this is me.
I am completely
one with her.

TRANSFORMATION OF PRESENCE INTO EXPERIENCES AND MEMORIES

Being acutely aware of the difference between a state of consciousness in which 'I' and 'my' world appear to be completely real, and a state of being where we directly experience the all-encompassing flow of being, we might naturally ask: "How does it happen that, out of this unified sea, the 'I' with its personal experiences is born?"

In our everyday life, we rarely recognize this deeply mysterious process which constantly transforms the presence into 'my' experiences and, subsequently, into 'my' memories. While living through the days of silence, my mind is struck, again and again, by this mystery, even as it tries to understand it, only to discover that there is no way to grasp it. How can I understand this double aspect of my existence? The incomprehensible presence is everywhere, without defined form, space or time; simultaneously and parallel to this, my entire personal life experiences unfold, changing from one moment to the next, like the scenes of a film.

What is the relationship between the two? And, what does it actually mean to have an experience? What is this mysterious process which seems to transform the incomprehensibility of the presence into recognizable and storable information, converting the unified flow of the Now into an experience that one has or possesses? Could it be that this is a basic aspect of the ongoing process of creation itself, where the unknowable totality and potentiality of the All manifests continuously in specific forms in consciousness, creating, simultaneously, the "experiencer" and the "experience" and a film that contains them both?

As the world crystallizes in 'our' perception, there arises, simultaneously, the recognition that we are an observer who apparently both sees and feels it. This happens in a flash, transmuting the indescribable essence of this present moment into a "known" reality of forms, sensations, images, words, feelings and identities. Ultimately, these might be nothing other than interpretations, projections or creations of the apparently perceiving organism – the famous Maya of the eastern traditions.

Are these the shadows
or the figures which cast them?
Evanescent forms
that come and go.
Are we the shadows,
are we the light?
The dance of creation,
dancing us?

The observer, who emerges together with the inner and outer worlds in consciousness, and who corresponds to our sense of a personal 'me', is not aware of this mutual interdependence of the seer and the seen but is, instead, convinced that what he/she perceives exists truly and independently of him or her. Yet in deep meditation, one has the distinct feeling that we are identical to our momentary experience; and that, in fact, we are nothing else but it. In those moments, when we are at one with the experience, we feel fully present and alive. Words, however, cannot describe that state. They can only point towards it.

Whenever something appears in perception, it is simultaneously compared with the contents of the brain's memory bank. Thus, the "something" is recognized and subsequently obtains meaning. The mystery of this biological process can already be seen in the instinctual behavior of very primitive organisms when securing their food or fighting for their survival. In us human beings, this process has evolved in a much more elaborate way. As soon as something is recognized, its form and significance takes complete precedence in the conscious human brain; so much so, that the formless essence which radiates from each appearance, seems to fade into the background. Within the context of time and space, the perceived is instantly transformed into something storable and is added to the memory bank as new information, like the photo of a sunset that gives the illusion of being reality.

All memories from our personal lives, and most probably, the whole of human history with its abundant knowledge, must have been thus collected in the reservoirs of memory and its "film archives". This process is at the root of our individual existence and has been deeply imprinted in each newly-born brain. In addition, this process becomes repeatedly reinforced through our education and our social and environmental influences and interactions, which persistently imprint the brain with modules on how to perceive and experience the world.

In spite of all these observations and attempts at understanding, I am aware that ultimately our analytical mind will never be able to affect or comprehend the core of life because the reality of life is far beyond it! It is nothing short of a miracle that we are at all able to consciously experience the wonders of life. How could we ever grasp this?

In the quiet
of the night,
all beings are awake
and dance.

All of a sudden – a snake! In a reflex, the body reacts and stops. The recognition process needs more time, as though certain switches must first be activated in the brain before it interprets the movement and I "know" it as a snake. Only then comes the fright.

YOU AND ME

There are these magical moments when you and I feel totally united in the presence. Carried together by the actual flow of being we no longer exist as a separate 'you' and 'me'. This experience of unison is the highest form of happiness we can share with each other.

We rarely encounter this graced state in our daily lives. Mostly, we experience each other as two independent individuals who meet one another with a certain known image of ourselves and of our relationships. We see each other through the filter of our shared memories and stories; stories from the past which are spontaneously triggered in our minds when we meet. The moment we recognize each other, we are in a sense "born" together. In a flash the identities of 'you' and 'me' – both inherent in this specific relationship – emerge and interact with each other. Only a counterpart, a vis-à-vis, can call us into this known identity with its corresponding behavior patterns. Though we experience one another as separate individuals, we belong entirely together. Like the two sides of a coin we are the two necessary elements of one unique relationship.

'I am' because 'you are' and 'you are' because 'I am'. You are my mirror without which I cannot see 'myself' as this specific 'I'. In each encounter with another 'you', a new 'me' appears in the mirror. This process, in which a specific identity pops up in the brain, can even take place when we merely think of someone, without meeting him or her in person.

Imagine for a moment that we are walking together as a couple on an early hot summer morning along the banks of a calm stream, absorbed in the play of light-reflections dancing upon the water. We are both completely entranced by the beauty surrounding us and the immediate presence. Together, we breathe it and are deeply moved by the shared experience that leads us from one moment to the next into unknown spaces – completely new, uniquely fresh and free of the past.

At that very instant, one immediately feels that whatever we can know or say about our relationship, including its memories and past feelings, has little significance for the fullness of this actual moment. Our intense shared history, full of its own beauty, pain and romance, clearly belongs to a different level of reality. It is the known "movie" of our relationship that has become dear to us and to which we are attached. This movie however, has nothing to do with the present reality.

When we begin talking to each other again, still sitting on the bank of the stream, we can observe how rapidly and unconsciously we jump back into this other, more familiar reality. Through talking we stimulate each other to withdraw attention from the mysterious space of the Now, and revert back to the world of our shared history with its familiar 'you' and 'me'. We resume the habit of communicating with each other as two separate individuals who are long known to each other and who continue to produce their shared movie. Most of the time, we identify so closely with this process that we are hardly aware of it taking place.

At any moment, however, we may step out of our film and contemplate one another and everything surrounding us as if for the first time. Our eyes open and we meet each other as a radiant presence. In this magical and timeless moment, we recognize ourselves in each other and experience that we are at one in this overwhelming reality of love.

You and me
we are one.

The shine of your eyes
is dissolving the world,
is melting me.
You endless lake,
you all-pervading
glow of love.

Without limits,
without conditions,
you are the beauty
of each soul,
you eternal light
in the sea.

From such a depth
you behold me,
that in your loving gaze
I drown.

TIME

The mysterious phenomenon of "time" is yet another important factor contributing to the puzzling process that transforms what is actually happening now into memorizable perceptions. Time surfaces in unknown ways in the fluid, timeless present, bringing with it division and measure. Time is the basis for the sense of continuity and permanence of anything that has been recognized as a separate entity. In that sense, time is, as the physicists say, the fourth dimension of matter. It is also our belief in time and continuity that gives our life story and our sense of self an apparent lasting reality.

However, when we examine this belief, we may see that, in regard to ourselves, continuity in time is a questionable concept. In observing our daily life attentively, we can notice that it consists of numerous separate moments like the frames of a film. In a flash, they each appear in consciousness; yet, in between them, there are many intervals of timelessness and discontinuity. Rarely do we maintain an uninterrupted thread of attention over longer periods of time. Rather, our thoughts tend to jump from one content to another, often without any connection to each other.

Each morning, upon awakening from a deep interval of sleep, where usually no 'I'-consciousness exists, we recognize ourselves to be the same person as the one who fell asleep the night before. In actual fact, however, each momentary identity with its sense of experiencing itself comes fresh into being in every new situation and dissolves again into the actuality of the Now in the interval that follows. If we are really attentive we can see that the conscious 'I' perpetually emerges and vanishes. What an ungraspable wonder of life!

Our psychological sense of time, our belief in the continuity of the 'I' is based upon memories of previous experiences and projections into the future. Most of our conscious actions, experiences and interactions are, therefore, embedded in time. Only in time are they "real", with meaning and continuity. In the present, they pass away even while they are being born. How could this ever be understood?

Nothing is born.
Nothing dies.
Is all a dream?

You drop a feather
over my watch.
Soft and light
it floats.
And time
stands still.

TIME, RHYTHM AND THE TIMELESS

As we dive into unknown silence and become frequently absorbed by the present moment, we become aware of how time and rhythm are a naturally occurring phenomenon in the mystery of Now. They simply happen, as themselves, within that which is timeless: time as time, and rhythm as rhythm. And often, time flows rhythmically: breathing in, breathing out, pause; dawn, dusk and night; Christmas rose, tulip, sunflower and aster; birth, adolescence, adulthood, old age and death.

In our daily lives, too, time appears in rhythms: the ups and downs of our moods – at times full of energy and then totally lame; moving from pleasurable to listless, from sociable to secluded, from painful to joyful, and so on. Simultaneously, while our state of being changes, rhythmically and over time, presence is always there, inclusive and all-embracing. One could say that presence is a stream, carrying within it the phenomenon "time", permeating it and endowing it with aliveness.

The rhythm of time is the rhythm of transience: emerging … submerging; appearing as form … dissolving into dust; becoming 'I' … dying as 'I'.

All that is manifestly alive appears in rhythm: the vibrating light, the multifarious sound waves, the oscillations of all elementary particles and force fields, fertility circles, and even the weather. Life's natural rhythms invite us to surrender to them and to allow ourselves to be carried by them. In their natural occurrence, they have a strengthening and healing effect. They cradle us, giving security and trust as they say – "yes".

Carried by the rhythms of life, we are happening together with time in the present.

Filled by presence
I transform –
into light.

You,
an imagination
and yet so real.
Like a form
that comes and goes.
A fleeting shape
in the tide of time.

Now – you are
an eternal song,
a distinct chord
in the chorus of all.
Flower among flowers
are you.
Unique – and yet,
to us alike.

Together
we are moved,
inspired,
animated souls.
Butterflies,
learning to fly
in cosmic space.

OUR BLINDNESS

Presence, the boundless essence of aliveness and of being, is an everlasting, unconditional reality. Its very nature is all-accepting and without any trace of conflict. Whatever happens, everything is immersed in its all-inclusive unity, within the totality of the Now. As contradictory as it may appear, even war, our practice of organized murder, is embedded in this infinite space of peace. All evil, terror and agony occur inside the present and are here at home. They are an undeniable part of the infinite realm of the Now.

However, when I sense this intrinsic unity, in which we all originate from the same source and are essentially one, the question inevitably arises: "Why do we ever go to war, and how is it possible for us to kill each other?"

The fact that wars constantly take place – that we torture, bomb and starve each other – underscores the dramatic extent to which we humans have gone astray. We are surely dwelling in a state of blind confusion and mental hypnosis, to continue committing deeds that so clearly reveal our growing loss of direct contact to life.

Only with a mind so disturbed and confused is it possible to put a belt of explosives around one's body and, full of hate and self-righteous conviction, walk into a crowd on a Sunday afternoon in order to blow up as many people as possible, including oneself; believing all along that this action will open the door to paradise. And only with such a fragmented mind is it possible to walk into a school with several automatic machine-guns and blindly shoot as many little children and teachers as one can.

Only in blindness can one sit with advisers and political colleagues in a comfortable office and decide, in detail, how to occupy a foreign country with our murderous military machinery – without considering the innumerable civilians and soldiers who will be killed as a result. And this all for the purpose of having even more power, even more money and presumably more security.

Only in a state of complete insanity can anyone declare with deep ideological conviction that a certain "race" of human beings has to be exterminated, ordering them to the gas chambers by the millions and killing them with systematic perfection.

How on earth is this possible? Why have we allowed this to happen?

Is all of this possible because, while I get up on a Sunday morning and prepare a leisurely brunch for my wife, and while you go with your children to church or drive to the beach, we both are utterly convinced that each one of us exists as a separate 'I' in this world; convinced that we are both leading independent, self-determined lives, and that all the shocking events in the world have little or nothing to do with us?

Is the framework of our identity so strong and the crust around it so dense that we can no longer sense the fluidity of our true essence, nor are we aware that the cells of the murdered and the murderer are flowing in our very own blood? Have we learned to defend our 'I' and our personal worlds to such a degree that our hearts have become closed, no longer able to feel that the breath of others is our own?

And yet, is it not plainly clear that in the presence of this very moment we all belong completely together and are inseparable? Is it not an indoctrination or mere imagination that our lives are disconnected and independent from each other?

But how can we – beyond all words and ideas – experience the actuality of our togetherness and live consciously in ultimate unity?

Is this not one of the most important questions we face in our lives?

How can this fictional 'I' and its imprisonment be illuminated and become visible for what they are?

What force could shake our walls and wake us up to our blindness?

What could touch our hearts so directly, flood us with compassion and open our eyes to this wondrous presence?

I lost my way
in this world
and wander about
like a madman,
unable to find a place
to finally rest.

I grope around
like a blind man,
searching forever
for the lost light.

THE 'I'-IMAGE

AM I AN IMAGE IN LIFE?

Sometimes, deep doubts and confusing questions occupy my mind when the realization strikes me: what I know about myself, what I believe myself to be, consists mainly of thoughts and images. My familiar 'I' is mostly made up of descriptions and memorized films of myself. Am I, therefore, just imagination? Are my past and my future, my wishes and fears, my body, my actions and my whole life nothing but images?

What is imagination?

It is useful to differentiate between the image and what it depicts. An image is, in itself, never the same as the reality that it reflects. Therefore, an image remains just an image. It is a representation, a translation, an interpretation. An interpretation is never the original "thing" itself. It is an abstraction, a model that does not breathe aliveness in the same way as that which is real. Representations always involve a process of imagination which solidifies the fluid and fleeting manifestations of life into what appear to be graspable and lasting constructions.

And yet, even if we understand this distinction intellectually, we nonetheless continue to believe that our images are a solid reality. How are we to grasp that it is not the image which is alive and that what is alive and real cannot be confined to an image? How can we absorb this truth so that it enters into our flesh and blood and shatters our deep-rooted illusions which separate us from one another?

It is a realization of which we are probably very wary. For, who are we if we do not believe in our own image? Is there a 'me' before or beyond the image? And, if so, how could it be experienced without describing it?

Born into being,
in front of each other,
we cannot let be,
and be who we are.

As images we freeze.
We search for a cloak,
and hurry to dress
when we see
how naked we are.

If I am not my story and not my memories, who am I then?
If I am not my thoughts and not my feelings, who am I then?
If I am not my body and not its sensations, who am I then?

Never the same,
always moving,
every moment
the new begins.

Never defined,
always all,
no need to know
who I am.

Any attempt to figure out through thought how it would be and what would happen if the 'I' were to disappear is utter nonsense. It is like using a flashlight to find sound.

MEDITATION

In the stillness outside, I listen to the movements inside.

In meditation, the attention focuses on being aware of the present moment with its changing appearances and on maintaining a continual contact with the presence itself. The intention is not to try to stop thinking, but rather to keep an awareness of the Now, even while one is thinking; allowing thoughts to be touched and washed by the presence, until they become as clear as crystal.

The coolness of the riverbed refreshes the brain. All around, the summer heat is burning the grass. The water, barely running, is singing a subtle new song. A relaxed awakening takes place as all senses listen; gentle winds, sunlit rocks and shadowy green. The body softly gives in to the swing of the hammock. The intense rhythm of the crickets suddenly stops.

There is no way out.
There is no way in.
There is only 'is'.

When 'I' am not,
there is being.
Then –
being is 'I am'.

We each carry our own inner cinema through the world. Together we sit – as separate movie theatres and audiences – in the present.

After the walking meditation, I sit down in the middle of the meadow. It is late August and the blades of grass have mostly dried out. Still, the meadow is covered with a sea of white lacy flowers and the green of wild fennel. I marvel at how each one of these hundreds of modest flowers is different and unique, together forming a floating tapestry of beauty. When they dry, they roll up into an exquisite basket-like pod that holds their seeds.

Out of nowhere, a butterfly with blue and red wings, perched upon one of these flowers, catches my eye. This unexpected impression spontaneously erases any sense of 'me'. It is as if I and all my knowledge, are blown away. There is only seeing. The butterfly, the flowers, the grass and everything around are united in the presence. No observer stands in between.

Pale the sun,
a farewell is near,
like the ocean
at a river's end.

Allowing me to sink,
like a falling leaf,
into the open arms
of this space.

Forgetting to forget,
forgetting to be.
All has ceased.

A rose petal,
falling next to you.
A heart in pink,
from dark to light.
Its time –
is over.

THOUGHT BUBBLES

Why do we believe so much in our thoughts particularly when they focus endlessly on ourselves, painting us in the colors of the past? They are nothing other than bubbles of air, drifting clouds of foam coming and going; self-inflating balloons, disguised in a bundle of wasted costumes. They are tireless tricksters and magicians, creating me and you. Let them happen. Let them pass by! The vast sky is untouched by the clouds that cover it.

Weaving,
weaving,
weaving the real.

Floating, floating,
floating as the real.

Arising
and passing.
In passing – arising.
Held by the void.

OBSERVING ONESELF

Nearly all our psychological problems and human conflicts are based on the habitual pattern of believing that the content of our thoughts reflects a true, reliable reality. In taking our thoughts seriously, we take ourselves seriously. Unaware of the dynamics of thought, we fail to notice that its content is dependent on our changing moods, on the environment or on associations and that its character is fickle, inconsistent and basically playful. Yet, even if we are aware of all of this, we remain, nevertheless, inclined to listen to the very next thought entering our mind and to the one immediately following it – especially if it evokes strong emotions in us. What we think and how we feel are constantly intertwined with each other, dancing together all day long. This dance is a normal part of our everyday lives. It is who we are.

One can learn to observe these processes without commentaries and judgments, in a state of accepting attentiveness that has no demands. When we discern the meaningful and emotional contents of thought from a distance and with a spacious mind, they become relative. Then they can easily be seen for what they are – bubbles, playfully emerging and disappearing.

   Once we gain practice in this art of observation, we can develop the capacity to shift levels of consciousness switching between being in a state of total identification with our thoughts to a state in which we allow the thought content to flow without resisting it or holding on to it. This does not mean that thought ceases to perpetually create the 'me'. Rather, the attachment to the meaning of thoughts that describe 'me' and 'my' situation loses power. The thoughts become lighter, having more space between them.

   With discerning observation we begin to comprehend how the sense of ego-continuity develops, and, at the same time, how unreliable it is. We recognize that the impression of our personal continuity is mainly based on incessant thought projections, describing 'my' activities and 'myself' in the passage of time. The 'I', consisting of memories from the past, is projected, as the actor into the present situation or into a future that does not yet exist. This projective thought activity is a necessary aspect of the planning and coordination of our practical daily lives. However, when our emotions and psychological problems come to dominate these film projections it is obvious that they have little functional value and nothing whatever to do with the actual Now. Thought-films are like clouds floating by. As interesting and amusing as they may be, they rarely bear any importance for the present moment. The 'I' may be seen, now, as it is: a clown or a painting that is constantly repainted.

Next door,
on the other side
of infinity,
you watch yourself
in the changing tides,
in the glow of stars,
and the deep red
of fading light.

You look at yourself
as a child sees a gift,
and are lost within.

Whether day or night
you fly with the wind,
and breathe the smell
of fleeting time.

Unsuspecting
you are
when then
it arrives,
the moment of death.

DUALITY

Duality means you are 'you' and I am 'me'; each one living in his or her own world, each one acting from an imagined independent center, each one conditioned by egocentricity and separation. Duality means that 'I' look at everything in the world – be it sensory impressions, feelings or thoughts – with the conviction of being a subject, the observer, looking at an object, the observed. This subject-object split is the basis of duality. The split occurs even when we simply think or talk about ourselves. The 'I', as the observer, looks at 'me' as the object.

The implications of this arbitrary split are enormous and completely dominate our lives. Our belief in judgments, our belief in categorizations such as "friends" and "enemies", or "beautiful" and "ugly", our belief in an "objective" world out there and a "subjective" world in here are all based upon the concept of duality.

However, if we observe ourselves throughout the day, we will discover many moments in which perception and the sense of being do not stem from a mind-set of duality. What happens in those moments? And what differentiates them from other moments?

Without noticing it, we are suddenly immersed in the immediacy of the Now – a space free of definitions or descriptions – without thought or inner dialogue. This can happen anywhere – in the supermarket, while we are sitting at our desk or in a concert hall. It can happen at any moment in our lives: while we drive our car, work on the computer or in the garden. These moments are so natural that one does not regard them as special. For a few moments we simply *are*, without thinking and without believing the content of our thoughts. Then, sooner or later, the 'I' automatically re-emerges and with it the 'me', the 'you' and the 'others'. These shifts in our level of consciousness feel completely normal to us, and we fluctuate from one state of being to the other, paying little attention to the movements themselves.

When we, however, begin to take notice of this constant switch between duality and non-duality, and recognize that duality is the basis of our psychological suffering, we might become more interested in and motivated to observe these transitions more closely. This leads directly to an exploration of perception: what is perception without an observer? What is reality without separated subjects and objects?

When the observer and the observed unite, describing and knowing cease. As there are no valid answers the questions dissolve. Silence embraces the mind and all conflict ends.

Clear forest pond
holding the source.
Drop after drop,
sacred water
is filling you
from deep within.

A fig tree drinks
out of your hands.
Its innocence
beyond all shame.

I dare to look
I dare to see.
In your silent mirror
the sun, the light,
reflecting me.

ON PERCEPTION

The other day, I read about a man who, having been blind since birth, gained the ability to see thanks to an operation. Contrary to all expectations, his new situation left him feeling completely helpless. Although his optic nerves were now sending signals to the visual cortex, thus evoking conscious impressions, the man, having been blind all his life, did not recognize the significance of those impressions. He, therefore, had first to be taught recognition.

This story suggests that we were most probably taught, and subsequently learned, to see the world the way we do. It indicates that individual objects, which we believe exist independently and "outside" of us, are not necessarily what we assume them to be. We can, therefore, presume that the world, as it appears to us, is a mere interpretation of an unknown "something" that is seen through our eyes – an abstraction created by the perceiving organism itself.

I am fascinated by the slow-running water of the creek as it glistens in the warm light of the late afternoon. I experiment with a soft, unfocussed gaze resulting in perceptions which are blurred, and I experience an almost magical transformation of the world. The unfocussed gaze transforms all movements, such as those of the leaves and branches above me, into fluid impressions in space. The forms themselves seem to be perfused by flowing energy, appearing like dancing gowns. With amazement, I perceive a moving aliveness in seemingly solid things. Form dances in non-form, emptiness in form, dancing with each other, concurrently. All solidity dissolves into a fluid reality.

Soon afterwards, while listening to the sounds of the crickets, hearing the noise of an airplane flying above and sensing the deep silence that follows, another surprising insight takes shape and it becomes apparent to me that thinking does not "do" the listening. Sound is to be found directly in the space of listening and not in the space of thinking. Upon closer observation of this astonishing phenomenon, I understand: in this space of listening, nobody is there to hear. There is only hearing.

Seeing is being.
Seeing is creation.
Through seeing itself
worlds are created.
The seeing of the tree
is the tree.

When one pays close attention to the processes of seeing, hearing, tasting or touching, it becomes evident that these experiences – where perception *is* and no one is actually perceiving – are quite familiar to us. There are many moments in our daily lives when we are naturally immersed in perception, often without noticing it. It is an intrinsic part of our nature to perceive without 'us' perceiving. It is only when we start thinking about the sounds, visual impressions, smells, tastes and bodily sensations – or even when we merely name or recognize them – that we believe, mistakenly, that 'we' are the ones who hear, see, smell, taste or feel them. But, in fact, this belief clearly belongs to the sphere of thought – thought that has nothing to do with the actual activities of listening or sensing.

Only in the realm of thought do we exist as 'I'. In all other realms of perception, the 'me' does not appear. When we recognize that we are actually quite familiar with these pure spaces of direct perception, we can appreciate how natural it is to be without the 'I'. In such spaces, all the beauty of the world is revealed to us, assuring us that there is nothing to fear when we immerse ourselves in the activity of direct seeing and direct listening. As we can observe in children, it is a most natural way of being. Lost in their toys, they play in the Now.

Right now, in this very moment,
we can only be,
where and how we are.
With no alternative –
whatever we do,
we are here.

WHAT IS WATER?

Water, as something distinctly definable, does not exist. For each of the sense organs, "water" as a phenomenon is something completely different and unique.

For the eyes, water is like liquid light; transparent, glistening, sparkling, clear or murky; running fast or staying still, forming waves, swirls and circles or smooth like a radiant, bottomless mirror; glittering dew drops on the morning grass, a rain shower over the land.

Water that is felt with the hands, or the whole body, gives the feeling of wetness, coolness, fluidity, of gliding through, cleansing, carrying and refreshing. With eyes closed, it is a whole new world of a completely different quality, possessing neither form nor structure – only sensation.

The sound of water opens up yet another unique universe. Sounds of water, water music; rushing, murmuring, gurgling, streaming; the rolling back of waves on a pebbled beach or their breaking on rocks; the downpour of rain, the trickling of an icicle; the sounds of water from the garden sprinkler or the sink's faucet.

Drinking water, smelling water: The salty ocean-water in our nostrils and mouths; a glass of cold water after hours of hard work; the smell of putrid water that stands still; the fragrance in the air after the long awaited rain.

All senses recognize water as "water", yet for each one of them it is something entirely different. The world of one sense organ can never grasp the world of the other. It is only by being related to the same source, and to the same word, that these worlds join together as something seemingly identical called "water". But, in reality, the same word is given to a multitude of different perceptions that only appear to be alike because of the name.

What is water then? And where is it? Is it in the eye, in the retina, or in a part of the cortex related to hearing or sensing? Or, is it, maybe, in those brain structures responsible for recognizing the different sense signals? Is the phenomenon, "water", simultaneously in different places? Or is it outside of us? If so, how does it evoke such different experiential worlds? What is the role of the senses? How are they related to what is outside? How can we ever know what is really there, when each sense translates and conveys it in completely different ways?

These questions are relevant not only for water, but for everything we perceive with the senses. To see a rose, to smell a rose – what unique and different worlds reveal themselves in one single rose! With such a variety of possible impressions, how can we determine anything which exists, as something "known"?

Even the instruments of measurement that we have invented can only make their observations from a given perspective, and capture only pre-defined parameters. The dilemma in apprehending what is being perceived can be expressed like this: "something" exists – however, through each of the senses it is transmitted as something different. Each one of the sense-organs draws from what is there and generates, in a lively and creative act, an appearance in consciousness which reflects the particular qualities of the sense organ itself. In this way, the senses take an active part in the dance of creation.

Finally, thought also has a function in perception. Thought gives these creations cognitive names and known attributes. The senses can only generate something as "known" once it is stored, through our upbringing and past experiences, as a concept or an image in memory. Similar to the story of the blind man, the legend of the indigenous peoples of Central America illustrates this fact, in recounting that they did not see the ships of Columbus, because they had no representation of them in their minds.

Upon bottomless oceans,
waves are creating a world
of dancing realities.

Beneath me,
turbid water
of milky mirrors.
From right to left
sounds are floating.
And in between –
the loud song of a cricket.

Not knowing
what is,
I bathe in
no thing,
that is all.

THE SENSES

"Were not the eye itself sun-like, it never could perceive the sun."

(J.W. v. Goethe)

What is meant by the word "senses"? And who or what is able to perceive them?

Beside their anatomical structures, the realms of the senses seem to consist of appearances that are created in, and by, themselves. Each sensory world is unique: the visual world, the world of sound and the worlds of taste, smell and touch. What we actually perceive are these "sensory worlds" and their content. Despite many discoveries made by researchers about brain cells, their interconnecting networks, and the correlations between aroused areas in the brain during the processes of perception, these discoveries provide no fundamental insight into the question: "What is the reality of the perceived and who is perceiving?"

The marvels of reality remain unknowable. They are an infinite mystery. Neither thought nor language with their definitions and conceptions, nor the senses with their different perceptive qualities, are able to unveil their secrets. In thought, as well as in sense perception, transmission and translation processes occur that lead to new creations. Their source remains mysteriously hidden – but is, nevertheless, always present. We are surrounded by it, yet are unable to grasp it for it neither exists, nor does it not exist.

What mystery today!
No cloud in the clearest of skies.
Deep and endless, the celestial sea.

Candle-like flowers, burning in pink,
are crying out loud.
Yet, the heat is standing still.

Nowhere a door,
nowhere escape.
Everywhere here.
An infinite,
echoless space.

SUBSTANCE

There exists only one single essential "substance". All is made out of it and manifests from it. While most living forms and structures appear to us to be different and, in themselves, unique – like a tree, a deer, or myself – we are rarely touched by the fact that their very "selfness" is made from this one "substance". All the billions of forms on this earth, including ourselves, are of the same essence. In spite of the numerous perceivable differences in appearances, in reality all is one. Since time immemorial, we have given many names to this "substance": "life-energy", "presence", the "eternal breath", the "Tao" or even "God".

Anything which is possible can manifest itself in many incomprehensible ways. Potentially, it is already contained in the infinite womb of creation, in the deep void of all space. It can be the most violent or the most loving act, the ugliest or the most beautiful form. It can be anything and everything. Yet, whatever it is, it consists of the one "substance" and is, therefore, in its essence the same as everything else.

Is that which manifests in a myriad of appearances therefore an illusion? This cannot be! "Shiva" or "God" has infinitely diverse faces and all are simultaneously real and unreal. Both the manifest and the non-manifest can originate only from the same source; a source which is contained within themselves as their highest reality. Everything which exists is a creative dance of pure beauty, the sacred dance of the essence of life. And in everything that exists, the creator and the creation are mirrored and witness each other.

Furthermore, the whole universe of thought, including the 'I', also originates and is constantly nourished by this original "substance". As a tree is nothing other than a specific appearance of this pure energy, so are all thought-forms with their specific contents.

Is it possible for thoughts to feel or be aware of the essential "substance" out of which they are made? Surely this can be only an intuitive premonition, a vague sense of something ungraspable. When in a moment of grace thinking is touched by its original core, thought becomes one with its essential self – and silently listens.

Nowhere is here.
A timeless beauty.
The lotus blossom
has opened her arms.

PHYSICAL FORMS

A form is a dance. Molecules dance. Atoms dance. The elementary particles which constitute them also dance as do the waveforms in their electromagnetic oscillations. Force fields dance in and with each other. That which is visible dances in the invisible, within a space pervaded by non-material information and intelligence. And all is dancing in a void and as a filled void.

All living forms and organisms are in a state of frail equilibrium which is continuously stabilized by a subtle act of balance. From a well of potentialities, complex vibrating formations arise throughout the course of evolution. Only temporarily are they gathered, joined and held together to form a specific organism, reflecting its genetic and environmental constellation. Enjoying a certain autonomy and self-organization, this organism is guided by an inherent biological self-preservation drive and lives, simultaneously, in constant communication, and fluid exchange, with its environment. The smallest particles wander as food from one being to the other, participating temporarily in the structure of this or that entity, while its body cells are in a continuous process of being assembled and destroyed.

In a similar way, we are all ceaselessly intermingling in our physical forms until, eventually, the personal "glue" of the individual form, the force that sustains its identity, loses its strength. As the structure becomes unstable, organism and form dissolve. That which constituted the prevailing stable form is once again accessible for new acts of creation.

Physical bodies are flowing, fleeting transitions – a wondrous stream of constant transformations. Only the actual aliveness, the presence of presence, is constant and unchanging.

How calm this night,

without a moon.

Only the stars are talking.

Stories of infinite space.

All doors are open,

taking us in,

and there,

in nameless peace –

are you.

THOUGHT FORMS

As with physical forms, the creation of thoughts and language can be seen as an evolutionary process of transformation: one word, one sentence, one language evolving from another. The basic material of language consists of sounds, words, symbols, meanings and certain semantic and form-defining rules. Out of sounds, words and sentences are formed which temporarily create meanings. These meanings form the basis for communication within the linguistic spheres of different cultural environments. Once again, a new "choreography" is emerging: the dance of vocabulary, grammar, and associations from memory. Sometimes, while listening to a foreign language without understanding its meaning, we may experience directly how the creation of all verbal expressions is a natural phenomenon emerging from the flow of life, like the song of a bird, a growing embryo, the flowering of the morning glory, or an approaching thunderstorm in the night.

Words belong to nobody. They take their course and perish. Every thought, including the thought 'I', is, therefore, a new and short-lived world. Similar to the cells of the body, the 'I' is constantly destroyed and renewed through these ongoing thought processes. Because this movement – with its repetitive rules and patterns – is occurring faster than one can perceive a sense of a continuous identity is created. Like the body, it appears to remain constant, day after day. However, both the 'I'-form and the body-form are perpetually coming and going, always being rebuilt. They only *seem* to be permanent, like the appearance of a standing wave on a river, which is nothing other than flowing water.

And yet, in spite of the two forms being nothing other than a sequence of fleeting appearances, we have become accustomed to believing that we possess a constant physical and psychological form which only changes very slowly, until it finally disintegrates in death. This is one of the primary illusions that we all share.

Liquid glass,
wind bubbles.
In the light
they reflect
our world.

When the solid
becomes liquid,
and the liquid
turns to vapor:
a million drops
are breathing
in space.

All existence is a continual flow, a multitude of movements. A tree is movement, water is movement; even a rock is movement. I am movement. You are movement. We are the movement of creation. We are the manifest world as it

becomes conscious. Everything moves together: clouds, thoughts, the human race. As one movement, we, together, are life itself. While we sleep, while we make love, while we kill each other, we are united as the creative expression of this moment. No way out, no way in. We and life are permanently one.

The whole universe is to be found in the shining presence of every leaf and every blade of grass.

The presence is the essence of this moment. It likens an all-encompassing flow that absorbs you, embracing you in the immeasurable quietude of infinite space.

It *is*, and that is its only characteristic.

To be is

to be,

and nothing else.

KNOWING AND NOT-KNOWING

Since all of our daily activities and interactions rely on what we "know" to be real, we have learned to develop an unassailable trust in our own knowledge. When we know something, we feel oriented and safe and hence tend to defend and argue over our so-called "facts". With the help of scientists, journalists, teachers and the Internet, we constantly expand our body of knowledge, and regard it as essential to drill our children to learn ever more. Where does this enormous importance, power, and so-called security in "knowing" derive from?

From generation to generation, we have been taught that the world can be known, and trust that we can acquire "factual" knowledge from reliable sources. Through habitual repetition, this conviction has been deeply imprinted on the brain, confirmed in every corner of our education system, and deepened by every one of our interactions.

Nevertheless, we cannot deny the fact that, our knowledge, with all its certainty, is limited, and that two crucial areas of our lives are inaccessible to our accustomed ways of comprehending – death and the immediate Now.

To know that one day we will die without being able to penetrate what that means: is that not life's greatest uncertainty? A constant disquiet lurks in the background of our busy days, as a subtle subconscious apprehension of the inescapable transience of our existence. And indeed, every day we witness the impermanence of our experiences. No matter how long we have been looking forward to something, before we know it, it has already passed by, and time between birthdays seems to be getting shorter and shorter. Looking at old photos of ourselves, we are startled and marvel at how young we once were, and when we meet former friends after a long interval we are astonished at how old they have become.

But, what really is the end? Very rarely do we dare to gaze into the abyss of not-knowing which death evokes.

When we are graced with the opportunity to sit next to a dying person and to observe how the breathing slowly fades away as the body sinks into non-motion, this mystery comes close to us, evoking a humble reverence. In those moments we witness such a strong existential truth and realness that none of our acquired knowledge can help us grasp anything and we are silenced. We sense the limits of what can be known and face the end of a personal story, a story suddenly erased. Something absolute is in the room that shakes us to the core. In that moment the certainty of our own end glares at us and puts into question everything that we know and do. An unrelenting question arises: "What really matters for me and what is truly essential during the remaining time span given to me?"

This last breath,
an astonished sigh.
The eyes wide open
in amazement.

The movement stops.
The body sinks.
An unknown bliss
transforms the face.

A peace from afar,
an otherness,
an opening
beyond all space.

I must let go,
let go of all –
even you,
my love,
when I dissolve.

Not being,
not not-being,
not nothing nor thing.

The same abyss opens up when knowledge tries to touch the present moment. Having never existed before, the Now cannot be known. It is always new, like an unknown, pathless land. To be touched by presence is like plunging from the known into the unknown. Instinctively, we cling to the known. Everything in us pushes and struggles to transform this ineffable present into something knowable. Yet, the Now is like a cliff or a crevice that suddenly opens. The next step leads us into nowhere. All questions about security and knowledge end here. Not-knowing flows into the arms of the unknowable.

No longer knowing.
No longer
wishing to understand.
Letting happen
that which happens.

Forgetting the future,
forgetting all plans.
And then –
forgetting my self,
within the stream.

THE CONSCIOUS FLOW

I AM HAPPENING

Everything transforms once it dawns upon us that the ego-processes are not generated or shaped by a separately existing 'I', but are occurring as an integral part of the flow of life itself. The key to understanding this basic insight lies in recognizing that the thinker, the actor, and the experiencer do not exist, as such but rather, that the experiencer is always united with the experience, just as the observer is at one with the observed. Awakening to this understanding is a groundbreaking process in consciousness.

It implies that, contrary to our innermost conviction, no one is separate or independent in their behavior. All conscious happenings are inter-related: they flow together in the stream of life, causing, triggering and conditioning one another. To experience oneself as an inseparable part of this prolific movement does not in any way diminish the wonder of life. Rather, it leads to a direct connection with the very source of life.

Just as body cells are generated via complex biological activities resulting from the intake of food, air and light, only to be broken down soon afterwards, so do the subtlest processes of the psyche surface and transform from one moment to the next. They do not happen in us or to us; rather, we are happening as them. For example, when there are feelings of joy or conflict in the mind, the 'I', with its sense of identity, manifests itself in this momentary gestalt. The 'I' in this case is not only inseparable from these feelings, but is, in fact, the actual expression of the joy or conflict, including all the physical sensations and mental images that accompany these feelings.

The 'I' is basically a life-happening and not a separate and continuous entity that leads an autonomous life. In each and every moment, the 'I' appears anew, in the form of the current ego-processes taking place in the mind and the body's actual physical sensations. Beyond these momentary processes, the 'I' does not exist as a definable entity.

These recurring and vital body-mind-processes, which form the basis of our "personal" experiences, are, simultaneously, an inseparable part of the holistic movement of the momentary present. Therefore, they are the expression of presence in its essential quality of 'I am'. The 'I am' is the sense of being, the original taste of life, present in all of life's creations. Our basic illusion or blindness lies in the fact that we take the essential 'I *am*' to be our personal 'I'.

It is this insight which ultimately connects 'me' and 'you' instantaneously with the All, and allows us to be part of it. Yet, at the same time, it is this insight which can evoke a feeling of complete dissolution, a premonition of the moment where we may lose control of the steering wheel: 'I' am not doing the swimming, 'I' am the swimming. While convinced that I am the one who is deciding and acting of my own accord, "my doing" is, in fact, the doing of life itself.

This double aspect of our seeming existence is extremely perplexing. It goes beyond any logical understanding to intuit that *'I' am an activity of life*. How can a subject ever simultaneously be an object and a verb, without the three being different? How can one move, be moved and be the movement all at once?

Delving into this paradox and the wordless truth that it points to leads to a state in consciousness which can be described as a floating equilibrium, a subtle, existential balance in which one is simultaneously defined and undefined, being 'somebody' and 'nobody' at the same time. Logic cannot fathom this delicate suspension in consciousness. It is disrupted the instant thought tries to grasp it. As a result, acute panic and confusion may arise in the mind and, like a cat trying to catch its own tail, thoughts go round and round in circles. However, once one gives up trying hopelessly to understand, a state of natural harmony with life's flow ensues. It is the embodiment of unconditional peace and acceptance.

Far above,
close to the clouds,
gliding circles.
Two buzzards –
messengers of power
in majestic flight.

As I point towards them –
they are gone.

WHO PERCEIVES?

An inevitable question faces me at this point: "If I am not the observer, who then perceives life's happenings and makes them conscious?"

It is difficult to consider this question without becoming entangled in new thought circles. The introduction of any new word as for example the word "witnessing", could re-trigger the illusion of a 'doer'. In order to witness, we immediately assume a subject who is witnessing. In this way, the word "witness" would be a mere replacement for the word 'I'.

As I contemplate this question, the activities of bee or ant colonies, which fascinate me, come to mind. These large populations live with their many complex coordination processes in great harmony, without a "conductor" at the helm who could be compared to a central 'I'. Instead, these colonies seem to be guided by an ungraspable awareness or consciousness which expresses itself in the flow of their manifold activities. The same is true for the complex coordination processes at work in the human body and in nature as a whole, as well as in the movements of the infinite stars and galaxies of the universe. Without assuming an all-pervading awareness and intelligence, how can we ever understand these inexplicable wonders of life?

We might, therefore, consider that the "witness" of all that is happening is "conscious awareness" itself, belonging to nobody, and free from description and comment. This "conscious awareness", with its ultimate intelligence, is an integral quality of all of life's happenings, including all ego-processes with their various features. Like the sound of the flowing creek and the waves of breath, all thoughts, feelings and sensations are a *conscious* life-happening, taking place in an aware space of attention. In a metaphorical way, one could say that presence, itself, is attentive and sees. Or one could say that "God" creates the world in order to become aware of "himself".

In light of this understanding, the assumption that we must rid ourselves of ourselves in order to enter the present – the concept of "ego-death" – appears to be absurd. It is entirely based on the idea of a 'doer', who can eliminate himself. When we begin to recognize the ego as a natural movement in the Now, sometimes very active and at other times inactive, it no longer stands in contrast to the present. Although the ego-processes strongly influence our subjective state of mind – giving us a sense of separation – they always exist as a part of the whole. Our banishment from paradise is an illusion.

Observing the sky
in a moonless night.
A million suns
in the darkness afar.
The space in space
is carrying us.

Shooting stars flying,
are glowing away.
How short is their life!
Looking in marvel,
all questions are silenced.
We rest,
we feel,
we are safe.

CONSCIOUSNESS

Consciousness – the visibility of the invisible.
Consciousness – the awareness of being.
Without attributes or dimensions.
Belonging to nobody.
It is the space and the light in which all appears.

Before all sound,
before all light
on dancing forms,
profoundest space
and deepest silence,
fulfilled by itself.

ATTENTION

States of consciousness depend on different qualities of attention. The question arises: "What directs our attention and what do words like 'attentiveness' or 'mindfulness' really mean?"

Normally, our attention leaps from one thing to the other, attracted by appearances – like sensory impressions, feelings or thoughts – that arise in the mind and take form in the field of awareness. Attention may also be voluntarily guided and focussed on something specific, such as reading a book, performing a task that needs high concentration or practicing certain meditation techniques. Both roving and concentrated attention belong to processes of the ego, unlike the impersonal "conscious awareness" that is an integral part of presence itself.

The kind of attentiveness that we are accustomed to has lost the connection to the present moment. It could be compared to the attention we give to watching a film in a movie theater, forgetting where we actually are. Though we may be attentive to our inner "films", we live almost always in a state of inattention towards the present. The moment we become aware of this inattention, for instance when we are directly affected by something acutely alive in our immediate surroundings, real awareness is aroused. This awakening abruptly changes the state of consciousness we are in. The recognition of inattention is, therefore, the key to being in the present.

Once inattention becomes aware of itself and transforms into attention, it can, without hesitation, let go of what has previously occupied the mind. In a natural way, thought-contents, with their emotional charges, lose their weight, giving space to what is here, to the awareness of the all-inclusive presence. Although the activities of thinking, sensing or doing, continue as before, the quality of consciousness in which they occur has totally transformed.

Perhaps the most essential capacity that we can acquire in life is, therefore, the strength to understand, as often as possible, the impact of the actual ego processes on the state of consciousness and the entanglements that ensue through inattentiveness. This implies stepping beyond the screenplay and seeing the film as a film while it is being produced.

As a guiding insight, this understanding might also help us answer another existential question: "What is our responsibility in life?" The word "responsibility" implies the "ability to respond". Rather than following conventional ideals and ethical concepts, our main responsibility may simply lie in the degree of mindfulness in which we live our daily lives. This entails being in contact and in resonance with all that is happening inside and outside of us. It entails being awake and therefore being able to respond directly to that which arises anew in each given moment.

When we open our eyes, alert and mindful, we shine and communicate in the present with our singular beauty. As everything is interconnected, we participate consciously in the holistic and harmonious movement of life, aware that we are happening within it. In this way, we can naturally blossom as the unique and lively being we are – with all the qualities, talents and personality traits that life has endowed us. Being ourselves, we are simultaneously united with all.

A gentle touch,
stroking the head.
Hardness dissolves.
Gateways open
to cosmic space.
All flows in,
streaming gently,
carrying us.

Then a silence,
a mirroring sea.
Darkness surges,
and nowhere ever
an inkling of sound.

All is listening,
all is swaying,
united
in creation's hand.

ALL IS FLOWING

Light itself is invisible, and yet it is the source of everything that is visible. The same is true of our world: the creator, the source, the original ground is invisible and only in its creations can it be recognized. The invisible lets the visible appear. To be witnessing, to be the "conscious awareness" in all that is and in all that happens – what mystery, what wonder! Light and darkness play with each other, and between them are the colors – the rainbow door between us and the one; presence and time, being and thinking, the unknowable and the known.

Sensing, listening, thinking, feeling – all is flowing. Thoughts are billowing with gushes of wind. Breath moves the walls of the body in a gentle, flowing motion. All forms, all appearances, all worlds melt into one: stone and sound, scent and light, water and air, all things, all beings and creatures, and the multicolored world of the 'I'.

Each moment is new, bringing with it its own particular flavor. What is is, and what is, is happening. Everything has its place: all nuances, all emotions, all forms and all extremes in each world. What is always there is presence, untouched by all. Each conscious moment contains the whole of all that ever was and yet, as itself, it is a unique and timeless new creation with neither a past nor future. Time and timelessness sit side by side. The present is happening and in it, time – the formless flow and the world of form. The formless shines out of the form as the intensity of being in its singular beauty – and its aliveness is presence.

The known world flows inside the unknown. I, with my past, my fears, dreams, plans and joys move together with you and all else through the unknown. We need not get rid of anything. We don't have to achieve or change anything. This can only lead us onto illusive paths. What we need is to see and to be touched by what is. The present with its presence is shining.

In order to see what is, we have to attend to it. This is only possible when our inattention and blindness become visible. They cease to be the moment they are seen for what they really are. And with that the seeming reality of all separation, which is the root of our suffering, comes to an end. Suffering results from division and time; it needs a 'me' that has an illusion of continuity. In the immediate present, all suffering ceases naturally and transforms into compassion. Pain and love unite.

Now is the present, is presence. Presence is not happening in life but rather, all that is happening occurs in presence. In itself, presence consists of nothing recognizable. While we human beings act out our lives, with its deeds and dramas, on the stages of our various worlds everything is made of presence. The Now is present even while we live in our memories, our stories and our films. Even when we lose our way, even when we fight one another, we are always in the middle of the flow of being.

You are this flowing present.
I am this flowing present.
Everything is.

Our path – as incomprehensible as it may seem – is always the right one. Together we are moved along it until we wake up, or die without ever awakening. To surrender to the flow is all we need to do.

Allowing oneself to rest.
    Pausing and listening.
    What most wondrous surrender!

We stop all our doing.
    The space opens before us.
    And everything becomes silent.

Conscious space touches the brain.
    With it comes presence,
       in all its fullness, in all its emptiness.

The lost son has returned home.

Carried by the stream of life,
reflecting joyful rays of light,
rose petals
are floating along
their unknown path –
and vanish away.

BRIDGES FOR DAILY LIFE

AFTER THE RETREAT

Most of us who have experienced a silence retreat in nature – either by our-selves or in a group – feel deeply enriched and grateful afterwards. There is no need to make a huge story out of it since throughout the retreats everything feels so natural, so simple. In the mirror of silence we come into contact with our innermost self and gain clarity regarding many personal and general human issues. We develop a sensitivity which tunes our whole organism to finer and subtler vibrations. Through slowing down, we acquire a new rhythm, and become more aware of the inner and outer movements that lead us from one activity to another. Above all, we are living much more in the present and in direct contact with nature, where the miracle of aliveness touches us deeply.

Having seen that the experience of the retreats strengthens us, that wounds were able to heal and many conflicts could be solved, most of us gain a strong motivation to continue on this path of listening and awareness of being upon returning to the "normality" of our daily lives.

With open eyes, we return home to our families, friends and colleagues, and perceive them often in new ways and with fresh clarity. At the same time, the various patterns of habitual communication between one another become transparent to us, and we find ourselves confronted with new and unexpected challenges upon our return. We realize that deep inside of us, a shift in per-sonal values has taken place. What appears to be very important for others has no longer the same significance for us, and vice-versa. Yet beyond those differences, we are acutely aware of the essence and uniqueness of each one of us, sensing our fragility, vulnerability and preciousness. This enables us to approach others more attentively, with understanding and compassion, allowing for more direct emotional and physical contact in our relationships.

Open the senses, open the mind.
How can I endure,
what enters and confronts me?

Each sensation, each impression,
every meeting touches me directly.
The wind as a being,
the towering clouds,
and you.
You move in me,
you swing in me,
and, thus, you are
a part of me.

How shall I show myself,
how shall I see you,
without a division
between you and me?
How can we meet without separation,
with porous skins –
and still be our selves?

However the return from a silence retreat unfolds, it becomes evident soon afterwards that, although we have experienced significant insights and inner transformations, the outer world has changed very little during our absence. Within a few days, we are unavoidably confronted with the familiar structure of our immediate environment and our society. We have to deal, once again, with its outer functioning, its patterns and routines, its stresses, its entertainments, its violence and its beauty. We realize that we cannot escape our world. We have to face it, function in it and accept it.

More than ever, we are aware that there are no simple solutions to our human problems. The clashes between nations, religions and ideologies manifesting themselves in wars, in extremism and economical exploitation, the gulf between rich and poor, and threats of ecological catastrophes seem to grow continuously. The trend towards increased alienation resulting from the evolution of technology, constant media manipulation and an all-dominating commercialization seems inexorable. What is more, the profusion of hypnotizing entertainment and easy-to-consume mental "fast food" is rapidly expanding, causing us to live a virtual "second life" with newly constructed identities, within a world of acquired fiction.

Meditative practices of pausing and listening, or contemplating basic questions about the 'I' and the processes of thinking, are regarded by many of our friends and colleagues as quite foreign, hedonistic or even absurd. How, then, can we continue our inner path of self-exploration in the midst of the habitual patterns of our relationships and the demands of our daily lives? How can we integrate the insights gained during the retreats and continue to practice the art of living in the Now?

These questions have accompanied me over many years, providing a fresh challenge every day. In the following sections, I wish to share with you some tools, practices and insights that have proven supportive and fruitful on my own inner path.

KEEPING THE CONTACT TO SILENCE

The greatest gift of a retreat – when all talking stops – is, obviously, the silence. With its calming and refreshing effect on the brain, it is the treasure we carry back home with us, affecting our way of being for quite some time. However, as this unique flavor of the retreat slowly fades away with each passing day we have to consciously maintain the contact to it in order for its healing power to linger and have a long-term impact.

A helpful practice is to incorporate daily reminders and periods of quiet contemplation into everyday routines. These can be short pauses in the middle of a hectic day, where we close our eyes and for a few moments, breathe consciously and become aware of being alive. Longer periods of meditation, different practices of body awareness and regular walks in nature or engagement in creative activities will, by themselves, connect us once again to the immediate Now. The main purpose of these practices is to sense and be continually aware of the real "taste of being". Through pausing, a release of attachments in the mind is possible and with it, an opening into the presence – into the space of silence.

Continual practice will undoubtedly have a strong effect on our daily experiences, our health, and our general state of being. As the "personal", ego-dominated space of consciousness comes into frequent contact with quietude and silence, strong identification processes, with their ensuing attachments, loosen up and become more fluid. These silent pauses remind us of our pure being and bring us into contact with our immediate surroundings. When we then resume our daily activities, an essential quality of this open and fluid space flows into our actions and shines through them. Subtle vibrations of silence and calmness are communicated from us to others.

The more we practice and experience this contact to silence, the more it is possible to find relief from daily burdens. As we enter into a lighter and more joyful way of being, our encounters and communications become easier and even difficult situations become more tolerable. To be able to stay in contact with the immediate present, even while being actively involved in challenging situations, is a priceless art to learn. It entails the conscious appreciation of intervals of awareness in which we mainly listen, sense and see, while remaining in alert contact with whatever is happening in and around us. In these attentive moments, we can observe how waves of feelings, emotions and thoughts occupy our minds, moving through the space of awareness and sinking back into silence. This allows the brain to be at ease, even in the midst of complex work situations. With practice, thoughts arise increasingly from a calm inner space. And thinking, itself, becomes spacious.

Slowly, it dawns upon us that, in fact, all our daily activities and interactions take place within this infinite space of the present, with its all-encompassing silence. We begin to see our lives – with their aspects of "right and wrong" and their emotional roller coasters – as a continuous movement of immersion in and emersion from silence. One moment we may be reacting to specific circumstances and dancing in our identity, while, in the next, we may become absorbed in silence. In lucid moments, we may even be able to observe these two states of being simultaneously. With silence as our friend, our energy, our relationships, and our contact to ourselves transform naturally. We become more attentive, loving and lovable.

Laugh from joy,
you wounded soul.
Pure magic surrounds you,
the magic that transforms the light.

You breathe from your heart,
and feel with wonder
that you are here.

All beings look at you,
and with their first glance,
they set you free.

These are your siblings,
everywhere dancing,
and their dance
is welcoming you.

Still, from afar
a memory beckons,
the memory of yourself.
A ripple you are
on this endless sea –
immersing slowly within.

TO BE WHERE I AM

The experience of silence shows us that the preciousness of life is to be found in the actual moment itself. The only place where we can actually feel our aliveness, with all its vital energy, is where we are right now. As we can only be in one situation at any given moment, it is inevitably the "right" situation for this time and place.

In order to experience this truth, we need to surrender ourselves to the given situation without resistance, without comparing it in our minds to other non-actual situations, and without wishing for something else. As difficult as this may seem we *can* learn to fully accept the momentary reality as it is. Conflicting feelings regarding the circumstance in which we find ourselves and our sense of separation then cease. Being in direct contact with the Now immediately alters the flavor of each situation. We are at peace wherever we are.

FLUID IDENTITY

Once we develop the practice of retreating periodically into silence and allowing regular contact to quietude and presence in our daily life, we can acquire a growing awareness of being in the flow of life. The 'I' with its thoughts, feelings and actions loses the quality of heaviness and rigidity that comes from fixed identifications. It lets go of what has passed and opens up to whatever is new.

Every day, upon waking up, the morning greets the world. The 'I' appears in consciousness as it starts organizing the day and itself. Awareness is there. In our first encounters with others, our eyes meet. When psychological problems or conflicts manifest themselves, with their emotional entanglements, we are now able to detect the specific dynamics and qualities of these processes. Once they are recognized, taking a few conscious breaths may be enough to reconnect with our immediate surroundings and with our hearts. In this way we learn to gradually disengage from our so-called problems. More space, more clarity enters the brain and we begin to intuit the appropriate action in any given situation. Spontaneous or light-hearted humor may often give rise to conversations, enabling us through our communication to connect with each other on an authentic level.

In areas of practical, functional and professional activities, many new developments may also ensue. As we grow to have less resistance and fewer psychological barriers towards our actual tasks, it becomes easier to deal with annoying and arduous chores in our lives. And when the "screws" in our brain are not so tight, a sense of flexibility develops, helping the brain to function more effectively. Often, unexpected solutions to problems, which until now appeared unsolvable, show up effortlessly. And, with less psychological stress, our work becomes more joyful.

Growing acceptance of life's happenings leads to a certain serenity. On such days, one thought flows into the other, one meeting into the next and one activity into the following one. The 'I' appears in every situation in a different form or gestalt and is more fluid, playful and adaptable. Occasionally, it feels as if one is actually carried through the day; at times intensely alert, while at other times quite lethargic – yet always with the dominant strong feeling of being where one is, and being with what one is doing.

LIVING WITHOUT DESCRIPTIONS

Is it possible for us to be here without describing ourselves, others or the given circumstances?

During the periods of silence we have seen that the world does not collapse when we no longer describe it, or when we, as observers, cease to see the world as separate from us. On the contrary, we are deeply enriched by those moments when the curtain opens, revealing the interconnectedness of all that is here. We remember that the brain becomes relaxed and at ease when touched by this togetherness. Without a center that is created by thought, everything is purely itself and breathes being. Inside and outside are no longer separate.

When we spend time in nature, with music, making love, or fulfilled by creative activity, we often feel at ease, free of descriptions and united with our experiences. How is it, then, when we meet each other in our daily work, while shopping in a store or enjoying a party? Can we also, then, feel this togetherness, without the need to describe and define each other with images we know, images which constantly create barriers between us?

To be able to live with such inner freedom is certainly a challenge, but it is also an opportunity which can lead us, even in our "normal" life situations, to seeing and meeting each other as beings among beings – seeing each other for what we are, without descriptions and evaluations. If we succeed in this, our relationships will improve, no matter how different our opinions might be. Even if only subconsciously, we recognize each other to be essentially the same.

SIMULTANEOUS PERCEPTION

Everything that happens right now is happening together as the living manifestation of presence. Yet, the capacity to consciously perceive what is simultaneously present in any situation is clearly difficult and unfamiliar to us. Most of the time our attention is absorbed by the particular details of what we are momentarily thinking, communicating or doing. For this reason we need to develop a conscious practice of "open attentiveness" that can teach us to become aware of the multiple things which are occurring simultaneously: current physical sensations and emotions, impressions from the environment as conveyed by the senses, the verbal content of our thoughts, or conversations with ourselves and others.

We can practice this art of simultaneous perception wherever we are. To begin with, we consciously recognize the various topics which are grabbing and absorbing our attention right now, and with which we are identified. Then, in order to gain some distance from our actual focus, we can learn to widen our visual field, thereby becoming aware of our immediate surroundings. The additional external impressions and inner processes that are happening at the same moment slowly surface in this open field of attention. As a result we can experience a renewed sense of pure being that is free of any specific content. This practice can be compared to the process in which a camera lens widens from focussing on a single detail to taking in a panoramic image.

Practicing this skill of broadening and opening our attention can be especially instrumental in difficult life situations. Widening the perspective can be likened to taking a deep breath and coming into direct contact with the Now. Everything can then be seen as interconnected and relative. Especially in times when we are completely caught by an acute problem or conflict, it is a surprising relief to awaken to everything else which is happening around and inside of us in that moment. It is like learning a new way of swimming – swimming in which one is performing a specific action and, at the same time, is carried along by all that is. It is a practice in which the focused and the unfocused, the detail and the whole, identity and beingness are all simultaneously perceived.

Allow yourself
to be seized.

Taking all in,
like a melting embrace
that you drink.

It carries you,
it streams through you
it sets you free –
through itself.

Open eyes transform the world
like a mirroring lake,
its waters reflecting the sun.

The light of love.

BEING AWARE OF WORDS

Part of the practice of attentiveness in daily life is observing one's associations and reactions to words and images. When we describe someone to ourselves or to others, we often rely on words which are loaded with stories of personal connotations and associations derived from past memories. Certain words or names are connected to experiences that we had long ago with different people in various circumstances. A certain name may, for instance, recall the memory of a pleasant personality and a happy event. Certain identifying labels like "rightist", "leftist", "millionaire", or "bureaucrat" might be loaded with a multitude of emotionally charged attributes and prejudices. In describing someone or something with such words, or by saying: "She looks exactly like so-and-so", or "This smell reminds me of the terrible kindergarten of my childhood" – we unconsciously attribute past associations and their connotations to the person or situation we are presently encountering. Believing that they actually have these projected qualities, we react emotionally – verbally or with body language – to these constructions in our mind.

When our present perceptions are so strongly tainted by the past, direct seeing and sensing is no longer possible. And often we do not recognize the injustice we consequently inflict on one another. In being mindful of this process, we can see how this programmed mechanism of projecting associations is the cause of many misunderstandings and conflicts in our relationships, distorting our way of perceiving the world.

The strong impact that deeply engraved associations to words and images have upon us is well known in the professional fields of public-relations, advertising and mass-media. There, we can observe daily how words and images are used or abused in a highly sophisticated manner to arouse our desire for products, to communicate information or news in a biased and manipulative way, or to paint and spread a favorable image of various influential personalities.

We can learn to become aware of our habitual reactions to such images and words and accustom ourselves to taking a few breaths before believing them. Thus we may gain the distance and the freedom to really listen and look into any given situation and to realize who and what is actually in front of us. It is only then that we may have the chance to react and answer adequately.

WE ARE WHAT WE EAT

What we take in becomes us.

A beautiful smile, a breeze of fresh air – they become us.

A video game filled with action and horror, a sentimental romance in the movies, a political talk on TV – they become us.

A delicious meal in a romantic location, a piece of lukewarm pizza at a stand – they become us.

Every single moment of the day we are absorbing something – assimilating it through the senses or through the mind.

An autumn-colored forest with the fragrance of late violets, a dance performance in YouTube on a computer screen surrounded by electronic equipment – they reach us through the senses, they spread through the mind, taking hold of us and becoming a part of us.

A concert in the cathedral, the squeaking brakes of our car, and the noise of machinery from the workers next door – they enter us, spread through our bodies and our minds and become a part of us.

A stiff business dinner with our competitor, a cosy family get-together in a forest lodge, a Facebook chat with our friends – they enter us, they take hold of us, and they become us.

All of our meetings, our communication with others, our entertainments, happenings in our workplace, all the people, moods and natural phenomena which we encounter during the day – they enter and become a part of us.

All the food, drink and drugs that we consume, spread into every single cell of our body, so that we are made out of them.

Whatever we read, whatever we watch, whatever we eat, whatever we talk about, wherever we travel and with whomever we spend time – we take it all in. It infiltrates the body and the conscious space of the mind. It flavors our sense of being. It becomes a part of us and we become it.

To be aware of this, to be alert to this, to care about what we take in, is to care for ourselves.

Looking back at our day, let us reflect: "What did we take in? What did we consciously or subconsciously swallow? What became a part of us?"
Did we have a choice? Could we decide?
Were we sensitive, observant and aware?
Each situation invites us to flow with it – or to flow out of it; following what feels right and what resonates with us.

Looking in the mirror at night, let us ask ourselves: "What took hold of me today? What was it that passed through me and became me?"
No judgement, no regret nor remorse.
Only feeling, sensing, listening.
Letting go.
Letting go – and opening all senses to the new.

A FLOATING BALANCE

When confronted with an acutely urgent question or an actual problem in our lives for which there is no easy answer or obvious solution, we can apply a practice that proved to be helpful during the silence retreats. It consists of allowing uncertainties and difficulties to float and drift consciously in the mind, without looking for an immediate way out but, rather, letting all possible responses and solutions remain open. Through this practice we can dispense with our natural habit of immediately occupying our minds with formulating, discussing and rejecting all types of answers. Instead, we allow the open questions to be suspended, unfocussed, in consciousness, without removing our attention from them.

When these open questions remain in silence, without triggering any intellectual or analytical activity, one could say that they are handed over to an "impersonal" space, a space in which all answers, still unformulated, are at home. This is the space of infinite knowledge and true intelligence which belongs to nobody and which guides and holds everything together in perfect order and equilibrium.

With this approach, thought and the ego learn to stop circling in intellectual and emotional loops of repetitive arguments and counter-arguments which only lead to dead-ends and utter confusion. Instead, thinking quietens down and the mind listens, with the question suspended in silence – listens until, at some point, unexpectedly and from an unknown quarter, an answer appears. Such an answer is often surprising and nearly always "right" – meaning that it does not evoke any sense of conflict or new doubts.

This path of calm inner listening, where answers arise from intuition and trust in a true intelligence, can be especially beneficial when we find ourselves in a deep conflict of contradicting interests and tendencies in which we try to balance irreconcilable relationships and situations, or when we are con-

fronted with the multifaceted complexities and incomprehensibility of life. In our lives we are so often attracted by different options and torn apart by contradicting desires. Confused by the impossibility of following all our diverse interests or trying to please everyone, we are left not knowing what to do. Some of our tendencies drive us forward in unbridled fashion, while others inhibit us through paralysis and fright.

In addition, we carry within us many secrets that we can hardly admit, even to ourselves: dreams, wishes, fears, embarrassments and unspoken words. We feel overpowered by intense emotions and by what appears unexplainable: the complexity and problematic nature of the whole human situation, the overwhelming intensity of life itself, and the threatening incomprehensibility of death. We are often tormented by what and how to decide, by what to do and what not to do.

In these situations it does one good to, once again, come into direct contact with the actual moment, abandoning all formulations, definitions and conclusions spun by thought. It then becomes immediately clear to us that right here, in the presence of the Now, the perfect balance and clarity that we are seeking already exists. In this space of equanimity, all our questions, longings, feelings of conflict or of being overwhelmed have their place and are held in the vibrancy of this moment. They are here and, therefore, they belong here.

Thus we come to understand that the sense of pressing urgency and the belief that we have to find solutions to our contradicting tendencies might be unnecessary. There may often be nothing to decide and nothing to be done. Maybe the task is to accept the multitude of possibilities, contradictions, dreams and unsolvable problems and let them simultaneously float and flow together as they appear and disappear in consciousness, without the need to act upon them.

Nothing is solid. Nothing is defined and permanent. Nothing has to be or ultimately can be decided. Sometimes it moves in one direction, then in the other, like a dancer on a tightrope. The realized and the possible, with all their potential, merge into each other, being essentially not so different from one another. To keep the balance, to juggle with all, to bear the weight of the undecided, to open the heart wide, to breathe with everything and to yield to the current of life – that is our task. Then, life is carrying us and whatever happens is right and allows for wholesome resolutions to evolve.

Thousands of arms
in Shiva's dance.
Kaleidoscopes in all his hands,
shimmering bubbles of the real.
Faster and faster the circles turn,
enchantment, terror, transience.
All swirls, glistens and bewilders,
arising and passing in the flight at once.
While Shiva – deep inside,
stands still and smiles.

OUR BEAUTY

There are times when we can let go of all our questions and doubts, cease our efforts to understand everything and simply live our daily lives, from morning to night, from moment to moment.

There is so much beauty around! To be aware of it! To be aware that we are not alone! To feel the love of our family and our friends! To see the joy and excitement of children playing, and the natural beauty which they bring to our world: their shining eyes, their beaming faces and their spontaneous tears! And the older ones: how deeply they touch our hearts with their fragility as they still try to participate as much as they can, their serene smiles accepting this last phase in their lives.

There is so much beauty around! Not only in the surprises brought by each season, with all its colours and changing moods. In every corner, wherever we look, we can discover something endearing: the way in which the young female cashier talks to us or how a stranger directs us to a particular address; the way in which we take care of our gardens, the way we dress, the way we enjoy a delicious meal. And all the beauty in the arts: making music together or listening to a concert in the cathedral; working for hours on a painting or a delicate sculpture; designing one's new home, organizing a cultural event; writing a novel, a scientific thesis, a poem, a letter of love.

How many moments of beauty in each day! Sunrise and sunset, a surprise visit from a neighbor, a discussion with a group of adolescents, a mother going shopping with her child. Seeing a movie about the wonders of nature, being invited to a party nearby, touching each other in a gentle embrace. Everywhere somebody is laughing, people are helping each other, and a new baby is being born.

It does not take much to see the beauty around us and it is not asking much to feel the beauty in ourselves. The way we are able to breathe and feel, the way we are able to walk, run and dance, laugh, cry and love: life is a continuous miracle! Night comes and the sky is clear, bringing the stars into our world and into our hearts: the infinite wonder of being.

LOVE

Love is a lover.
Love is a flower rejoicing in her beauty.
Love is the presence of you in me.
Love is a child who for the first time sees.
Love is the light in every form.
Love as a lover dissolves all form.
Love is a hand that holds you in dying.
Love infuses the fragrance of life.
Love is a stream that knows no time.
Love is the end of all beginnings.
Love is the essence, the eternal sea.

When we feel love, when we see and experience the people around us with love, we feel unquestionably connected to our natural state of being. Through itself, love brings us into direct contact with the essence of life and the unifying stream of presence. Presence is love and everything is presence. Love is not an attitude that we can or must acquire or cultivate in our daily lives. Love is like a lake in which we are always swimming and which swims in us. When we feel it, we feel real.

FREEDOM AND RESPONSIBILITY

Interwoven with everything, we – with all our experiences – are happening within life's happening. Every moment of our daily lives, every action and event is a specific expression of innumerable elements that condition, define and trigger each other. All that happens, all that is manifest, springs from the same source. Everything in the perceivable world is occurring together as one unified present movement. Nothing happens solely through any singular cause or through any single person like 'you' or 'me'. No activity seemingly performed by the 'I' is actually 'my' action – it is always life's activity.

Nevertheless, over and over again, the pensive and restless mind confronts us with the question: "Does this mean that we are just a pawn in the play of forces, deprived of any free will, a cogwheel in a karmic-cosmic machine? Do we not have responsibilities in our lives? Do we not have choices?"

As we go deeper into these questions, contemplating different situations in our own lives, we can find out that there are many possible answers and that each answer depends completely on the state of consciousness from which it arises.

In a state of consciousness that is filled with the reality of pure presence, any question is, in itself, senseless. It is just a sequence of abstracted terms placed next to each other without any real meaning. Concepts like "will", "choice" and "responsibility" as terms dissolve completely in the flowing reality of Now, of *being*. Where there is no separation and no 'me', who could be responsible for what is taking place?

In a state of consciousness in which 'I' and 'the others' are experienced as distinct from each other, yet with the awareness that we are sharing the same life-movement and are together at each moment, the answer may be as follows: Because I am connected to everything, my thoughts, feelings and actions influence everything. Therefore, my state of being and my personal aura are a continuous contribution to the overall happening of this moment. My rage, my resentments, my fears, my joys, my pleasure and my love expand in all directions, and these energies affect all that is close to me. My violence clearly increases violence around me, my negativity augments negativity, my joy adds joy to the moment and my compassion and love reinforce compassion and love. I am responsible for the "fragrance" that I contribute to each present moment through my way of being.

In a third possible case, the 'I' feels itself to be in a state of clear separation. The 'I' assumes it is acting in the world as an independent, autonomous entity. In this state, 'I' clearly must believe that I have a free will, have choices and am, therefore, responsible for my actions. Good and evil, guilt and forgiveness, and all ethical and moral convictions appear, therefore, to be part of my world. Depending on my psyche and my character, these ideological convictions might often put me into conflict, or push me to be a better, morally superior human being. In order to gain stability in my life, I will have to develop a well-defined self-image and will continually try to control 'my' life through making "right" decisions.

And then there is the fourth possibility of feeling that I am a separate 'me' whilst, at the same time, being a victim of karmic or other circumstances, suffering passively throughout life, unable to help 'myself'. In this case 'others', my unfortunate destiny or bad karma from a former life are responsible for everything that is happening to me, leaving me with no choice.

Reflecting upon these four different states of consciousness and the different realities and paths through life that they imply, we might ask: "Is there one 'right' path or are they all 'right' or maybe all 'wrong'; and what can guide us, and give us clarity?"

A colorful spider caught a wasp in her web.
Holding it with her long legs,
she patiently eats it.
As the wasp disappears,
it becomes her.

Exploring these questions is, for some of us, an inner process which continues throughout our lives. While observing ourselves over the years, we might find that it is almost impossible to escape from our personal make-up. The conditioning of the 'me' proves to be very solid and effective. Although some expressions might change, the basic traits and tendencies remain dominant in our behavior. And yet, it is crucial to realize that every moment is new and offers us a variety of ways in which to appear and conduct ourselves in the world. What, then, determines how, as whom and with what behavior, and flavor we become visible and act in the world?

It seems self-evident to me that our inner state and our outer appearance and behavior depend largely on the degree of mindful attention we give to the actual inner and outer happenings and, above all, on the direct contact we have with the living presence. Choice lies in the always-available option and opportunity to direct our attention towards this direct contact. Life is constantly calling us and talking to us. We have the freedom to hear the call, to observe, to listen, and to be moved by it. We are always free to decide where to direct our attention and with what content to fill our conscious mind.

Through attention, the senses open up and connect to the space which holds everything that occurs. The horizon widens and, in most situations, a variety of realities and behavioral possibilities present themselves so that what is most fitting for each moment appears and happens quite naturally. Out of open attentiveness – perceiving content and context together – genuine actions arise spontaneously that are balanced and in harmony with what is. Our behavior, our presence and our way of relating are basically in tune and are, therefore, appropriate and authentic. There are no mistakes.

Each moment presents the challenge and opportunity to consciously practice achieving this sensitive balance: on the one hand, to actively turn one's attention towards the actual, to perceive what is happening and to be able to respond; and, on the other hand, to simultaneously surrender, without any resistance, to the flow, and give in to what is. This requires a constant, conscious practice of attentiveness, of listening and acceptance – with patience. It requires the freedom to simultaneously be 'somebody', 'nobody' and 'all'.

In this way, we walk – or "are walked" – through the world and through life, having an identity and having no identity, acting as 'me' and being the action of 'all' in this very moment. Sometimes the 'others' appear distinctly separate from 'me', while, at other times, we all are suddenly united in the activity of the Now. And – always and everywhere – there is presence. 'I' am presence. 'You' are presence. All is presence.

Presence is the invisible, ungraspable, indescribable source, essence and reality of all. It is beyond form and non-form. It is beyond any category or description. Presence dances the dance of all manifestation. Presence dissolves all manifestation.

Now, the beauty of our essential being shines, and we are a light in the light. Whatever happens, wherever the winds blow or the tides shift – we are at home.

Surrender yourself,
you,
a song of light.
Surrender now,
to the flowing sounds
and the stream of silence,
from where you sing.

Appendix

STRUCTURE OF THE SILENCE RETREATS
IN POCI / TUSCANY

The silence meetings in POCI are open for all who wish to experience a period of silence within the accepting and supportive atmosphere of a group. They have no ideological or traditional religious orientation.

The retreats last from 7 to 14 days, with a group of 8 to 16 people. The first day of each retreat is dedicated to introductions, answering questions, exchanging views on meditation, perception, mental and emotional processes, and clarifying all practical details. The intention is to instill a sense of security and a feeling of being at home before commencing the days of silence.

The silence retreat ends with a day of integrating group dialogues, in which we share our experiences and prepare for the return to daily life. During the retreat we offer the option to participate in 4 daily meditations. Weather permitting, we use different spaces in nature for walking and sitting meditations. Participants are free to follow their individual meditation practices.

A communal vegetarian dinner is served in the evening. Each participant prepares his or her own breakfast and lunch. Once a week we practice a day of slow-motion. Gentle breath sessions may be scheduled during the retreats.

More information about the silence retreats can be found at:
www.locpoci.com

LIST OF RELATED BOOKS

ATABAY, CYRUS (TRANSL.):
*Hafis, Rumi, Omar Chajjam –
Die schönsten Gedichte aus dem
klassischen Persien.* C.H. Beck,
Munich, 2nd ed. 2004

BARKS, COLEMAN WITH MOYNE,
JOHN (TRANSL.): *The Essential
Rumi.* Harper, San Francisco 1997

BOHM, DAVID: *On Dialogue.*
Routledge, London 2004

BOHM, DAVID: *Thought as a
System.* Routledge, London 1994

BOHM, DAVID/PEAT, DAVID F.:
Science, Order and Creativity.
Bantam, New York 1987

CAPRA, FRITJOF: *The Web of Life.*
Anchor Books Doubleday, New York
1997

DÜRR, HANS PETER/
ÖSTERREICHER, MARIANNE:
*Wir erleben mehr als wir begreifen.
Quantenphysik und Lebensfragen.*
Herder Spektrum, Freiburg, 6th ed.
2006

DUNN, JEAN (HG.): *Prior to Consciousness. Talks with Sri Nisarga-
datta Maharaj.* Acorn Press,
Durham/North Carolina 1990

MEISTER ECKHART: *Deutsche
Predigten und Traktate.*
Hanser, Munich, 6th ed. 2000

FOERSTER, HEINZ VON/
GLASERFELD, ERNST VON/
HEJL, PETER M./SCHMIDT,
SIEGFRIED J./WATZLAWICK, PAUL:
*Einführung in den Konstruktivis-
mus.* Piper, Munich/Zurich, 9th ed.
2006

GODMAN, DAVID (HG.): *Be as you
are. The Teachings of Sri Ramana
Maharshi.* Arkana Penguin, Lon-
don/New York 1991

HAYWARD, JEREMY:
*Die Erforschung der Innenwelt.
Neue Wege zum wissenschaftlichen
Verständnis von Wahrnehmung,
Erkennen und Bewusstsein.* Insel
Taschenbuch, Frankfurt am Main
1996

KABIR: *Im Garten der Gottesliebe.*
Werner Kristkeitz, Heidelberg 2005

KRISHNAMURTI, JIDDU:
The Awakening of Intelligence.
Harper, San Francisco 1987

KRISHNAMURTI, JIDDU:
Freedom from the Known.
Harper, San Francisco 1975

KRISHNAMURTI, JIDDU: *Krishnamurtis Notebook.* Krishnamurtis
Publications of America, 2004

KRISHNAMURTI, JIDDU/
BOHM, DAVID: *The Ending of Time.*
Harper, San Francisco 1985

LAOTSE: *Tao Te Ching. A new English Version by Stephen Mitchell.* Harper Perennial, New York 1991

LASZLO, ERVIN: *The Connectivity Hypothesis. Foundations of an Integral Science of Quantum, Cosmos, Life, and Consciousness.* State University of New York Press, Albany 2003

LASZLO, ERVIN: *Science and the Akashic Field. An Integral Theory of Everything.* Inner Traditions, Rochester/Vermont 2007

LASZLO, ERVIN: *Science and the Reenchantment of the Cosmos. The Rise of the Integral Vision of Reality.* Inner Traditions, Rochester/Vermont 2006

MITTELSTEN SCHEID, DIETER: *Türen zum Sein.* Eigenverlag, Munich 2002

RICHTER, HERTA/MITTELSTEN SCHEID, DIETER: *Vom Wesen des Atems.* Forum Zeitpunkt Reichert, Wiesbaden 2006

RILKE, RAINER MARIA: *Gesammelte Werke, Band 1 und 2 Gedichte.* Insel, Frankfurt am Main 2003

SIEFER, WERNER/WEBER, CHRISTIAN: *Ich. Wie wir uns selbst erfinden.* Campus, Frankfurt am Main/New York 2006

SINGER, WOLF: *Ein neues Menschenbild? Gespräche über Hirnforschung.* Suhrkamp Taschenbuch, Frankfurt am Main, 4th ed. 2006

SRI NISARGADATTA MAHARAJ: *I am that.* Acorn Press, Durham, 2nd ed. 2012

STARKMUTH, JÖRG: *Die Entstehung der Realität. Wie das Bewusstsein die Welt erschafft.* Goldmann Arkana, Munich 2010

SUZUKI, SHUNRYU: *Zen Mind Beginners Mind,* Weatherhill, New York/Tokyo 1973

VARELA, FRANCISCO J.: *Ethical Know-How.* Stanford University Press, Stanford 1999

VARELA, FRANCISCO J.: *Traum, Schlaf und Tod. Grenzbereiche des Bewusstseins. Der Dalai Lama im Gespräch mit westlichen Wissenschaftlern.* Piper, Munich, 5th ed. 2005

WILBER, KEN: *Quantum Questions. Mystical Writings of the World´s Great Physicists.* New Science Library. Shambala, Boulder & London 1984

ABOUT THE AUTHOR

Born in 1942 in Munich, Germany, Dieter Mittelsten Scheid is a medical doctor, psychotherapist and breath-practitioner. He trained in psychiatry and humanistic psychotherapy, as well as in breath-therapy with Herta Richter and in Feldenkrais functional integration with Alon Talmi. In his spiritual development he was deeply influenced by Jiddu Krishnamurti, and experienced the practice of Vipassana Meditation with S.N. Goenka. He was co-founder of the "Coloman Zentrum", a center for humanistic psychotherapy east of Munich, where he worked as a therapist from 1972 to 1982. For the past 30 years he and his wife Batya Schwartz have been leading silence and consciousness retreats at their center, "POCI-Retreats" in Tuscany.

Throughout my training as a medical doctor, as a therapist and later as a practitioner of body- and breath-work, I have always been searching for that which would bring me into direct contact with life itself. Increasingly touched by the growing estrangement and insensitivity in our society, I have been searching for natural ways to re-connect to our essence, to each other and to the intrinsic beauty of life. Living close to nature on a farm in the wooded hills of Tuscany, I have been fortunate to spend a considerable amount of time together with others in silence. These retreats into silence have enriched and inspired me, filling me with gratitude. They have given me the opportunity to study our human mind with all its strain, confusion and potential, and to experience, over and over again, how all problems dissolve when the brain is touched by the immediacy of the Now – where one is taken in by the flowing movement of the presence.